A Christian Guide to Liberating Desire, Sex, Partnership, Work, and Reproduction

Thia Cooper

A Christian Guide to Liberating Desire, Sex, Partnership, Work, and Reproduction

palgrave
macmillan

Thia Cooper
Department of Religion
Gustavus Adolphus College
Saint Peter, Minnesota, USA

ISBN 978-3-319-70895-9 ISBN 978-3-319-70896-6 (eBook)
https://doi.org/10.1007/978-3-319-70896-6

Library of Congress Control Number: 2017959108

Cover illustration: Pattern adapted from an Indian cotton print produced in the 19th century

Printed on acid-free paper

This Palgrave Pivot imprint is published by Springer Nature
The registered company is Springer International Publishing AG
The registered company address is: Gewerbestrasse 11, 6330 Cham, Switzerland

To Raoul

PREFACE

As a liberation theologian and Professor of Religion and Latin American Studies, I did not expect to write about sex. Yet, here I am. As a liberationist, I was initially focused on the various forms of poverty I saw around the world. I wanted to educate students on these forms of poverty and how religion could help us to work toward a more just world.

I began teaching at Gustavus Adolphus College, a small liberal arts college in Minnesota. Here, I quickly found myself flummoxed by MANY conversations with students about sex and relationships. While I had avoided all things personal with my college professors, these students had lots of questions and wanted help. I found myself in several conversations, including the following:

> I'm pregnant. Should I get an abortion?
> I got an abortion but it didn't work.
> I think I was raped last night.
> I was raped last night, but it was my fault.
> I'm afraid I may have raped my girlfriend.
> I don't like my boyfriend but he doesn't make me have sex.
> I think I'm bi-sexual.
> I had sex with him because he paid for our weekend away.

Now, I don't know about you but I was NOT trained to coherently converse about any of these things. Mainly, I listened. And I thought about what I had learned growing up. And I read, A LOT. I also started teaching a class called Sex, Race, Money, God. As I read and taught,

I found many intersections between race, class, sex, and sexuality. I found many articles I could share with my students but I could not find a text that overtly explored how to have good sex from a Christian perspective. I could also not find a text that had a coherent framework, which applied to desire, sex, partnership, and reproduction. And even the few that discussed two or three of these avoided sex work like the plague.

So, here we are. I hope that this book helps you begin to think about how to have just sexual relationships.

I am so grateful to my students for sharing their experiences with me. Between the great students in my classes and those I lived with for three years as Head Resident of the International Center on campus, I learned how to navigate difficult conversations, laughing and crying, usually at the same time. I am also grateful to my colleagues at Gustavus, many of whom read bits and pieces of this work and, in particular, encouraged me to keep going every time I freaked out about writing a book about sex. I am grateful for the wonderful sexual experiences I have had and for some of the less wonderful experiences, as I learned how to have good sex from those as well. Without naming names, several people have taught me about friendship and sex and this book could not have been written without them. Last but not least, I want to thank my mother for her love and support. She got married at age 70 and promptly paid me back for all my openness about sex in my teenage years by sharing way too much about her new love life.

Saint Peter, MN, USA — Thia Cooper

Contents

1 Introduction: Liberating Sex 1

2 Desire 23

3 Sex 35

4 Partnership 57

5 Sex Work 79

6 Reproduction 93

7 Conclusion 111

Definitions 113

Further References 115

Index 119

CHAPTER 1

Introduction: Liberating Sex

Abstract Each time we have sex, God is present. Sex can be a way to know God. This introduction articulates how liberation theology and its method can help to rethink the Christian tradition's denigration of sex and desire. Beginning with the current situation around sex, in particular, an understanding of the body, power, and violence, the chapter explains how we can work with the Bible, Christian tradition, and theology to liberate sex.

Keywords Desire • Sex • Partnership • Power • Violence

Why liberate sex? How is sex enslaved, unjust? Each time we have sex, God is present. Sex can be a way to know God. People often say it's "just sex." Well, let's unpack what just sex is. Those of us within the Christian tradition do not often discuss just sex. This book does. Liberating sex brings us closer to God. Students seem to think Christianity simply says "no sex before marriage." Instead, I want to urge us toward a positive sexual theology. How can sex lead us to justice?

I care about just sex because I believe we come to know God through knowing others. If our relationships with others are unhealthy, then we are not learning about the true God. Sex is one way people relate and sex is a place where God is present, even if, in the words of one of my students,

T. Cooper, *A Christian Guide to Liberating Desire, Sex, Partnership, Work, and Reproduction*,
https://doi.org/10.1007/978-3-319-70896-6_1

"I don't like to think about God when I'm doing that." Yes, it can be scary to figure out what our relationship with God looks like.

I'll begin with the actual sexual practices of human beings. Predominant Christian theologies argue that sex should only occur between a man and a woman within the bounds of marriage. This argument excludes the majority of people having sex. Growing up, Christianity taught me not to discuss or have sex, the end. But if we don't talk about what good sex looks like, then it is unsurprising we also have a hard time articulating what bad sex is. We need to uncover the theology underlying actual sexual practices. Then we need to make sex just. From within Christian theology, I ask how we can love God and love sex. The sexual landscape is constantly changing. If the boundaries of what defines "sex" were porous before, they barely exist now. Thus, this theology is of the bedroom, Skype, a massage parlor, any place we exist.

To have a just sexual relationship power must be shared, empowering the participants and the wider community. We are speaking of individual relationships and the very structures of society. We do so considering the humanity of each human being in the community.

Donna Freitas[1] wrote a wonderful and depressing book called *Sex and the Soul.* It provides evidence for the desperate need for holistic sex education. As we know, students separate religion from sex, unless evangelical; then it's no sex or even kissing before marriage. The book details these facts.

> Both Catholic and mainline Protestant … students laughed out loud when asked what their faith tradition might have to say about these matters. … They laughed because they see religious views about sexuality (at least what they know of them, which is typically not very much) as outdated and irrelevant. And they laughed because they were confused about the prospect of their faith having anything useful to say about these things. (Freitas, 196)

What Is Theology and How Can It Help?

This book "does" theology, exploring how we can have good sex within Christianity. Theology can be defined as "faith seeking understanding." Here, faith seeks to understand how we know God through our sexuality and sex lives. "Seeking" here must include action, not simply thinking or talking. We can say what we like about sex but our actions show our true theology. In examining faith/theology, we often look to scripture and tradition along with our experience and "reason." Helpful questions and analyses emerge from many theologies, particularly liberationist theologies: queer, feminist, womanist, black, economic, political, ecological, and so on. I'll explain a few of these here.

Latin American liberation theology emerged in the 1960s within Catholic communities of poor people. These poor Christians began to articulate that God was on the side of the poor. From these communities emerged a theology that expanded across the globe. Liberation theology prioritizes the marginalized, people usually excluded from the conversation, and it prioritizes action. Most importantly, liberationists subject everything to suspicion, rethinking and reflecting on faith and action. In this book, I prioritize people most excluded from the conversation.

Liberation theologies argue that Christianity should free people to be full human beings. Our sexual theology needs liberation. Liberationists argue that we should work toward God's kingdom, the new heaven and new earth where justice will rule. Liberation theology asks who should we partner with, can we sell and buy sex, who can have children, and so forth, and combines aspects of race, economics, politics, gender, sexuality, religion, and so on.

Feminist theology resists the marginalization of women, calling for equality in practices and structures. Rather than assuming theology is neutral, feminist theology realizes that patriarchy, which places men at the top of the power spectrum, has influenced theology. Feminist theology aims to rethink Christianity, rescuing it from patriarchal assumptions. Ecofeminist liberation theology resists the marginalization of the environment as well, articulating that all of nature is sacred. The environment affects us all, whether poor or rich, black or white, male, female, and everything in between.[2] Ecofeminist theology urges us to consider the inescapable fact that we are intertwined with our environment. Women are often the caretakers of children and are often the ones surviving in hostile and damaging environments. There are also womanist, Latina, and other theologies from women of color, excluded from the original feminist theologies, which tended to reflect the themes of white middle-class women.

Finally, sexual theology begins with the notion that we are sexual beings. This theology assumes sexuality is part of our lives. This is the newest strand of liberation theology and the emphasis of this book.

How Will I Tackle This Topic? (Method)

Traditionally, the areas influencing theology are divided into a quadrilateral: scripture, tradition, reason, and experience.[3] Scripture is the sacred text of any religious tradition. In this book, we use the Christian Bible. Tradition is the history of one's religion, theologians and ethicists, and religious doctrines or dogma (right rules). Reason is thinking rationally or academically; hence it includes academic subjects from psychology to economics. Experience is what we learn through our daily lives.

Liberation theology follows a slightly different method known as the hermeneutical (interpretive) circle. This circle blends action and reflection together in community. As a liberation theologian, I try to draw together threads of theology emerging from these communities. Its simplest form is "See-Judge-Act."

The first step in the circle is a process of self-awareness, called conscientization. It is becoming aware of our situation and how that situation sits in history and culture: See. We do this work in community; it relates to the concept of experience mentioned earlier. Differently though, it is not the experience of one person but a community together. Recognizing our own situation is the first step to analyzing and improving it. Why and how are we sexually impoverished?

The next step is to analyze the situation with all the academic tools at our disposal: Judge. We can analyze using the academic tools of economics, politics, sociology, race studies, sex and gender studies, and so on. This step is similar to "reason" described earlier.

The third step is to analyze the situation with all the theological tools at our disposal, while at the same time analyzing the theology itself: Judge. We can analyze our faiths, whether Christian, Muslim, Jewish, and so forth, to find the underlying theologies of sex and sexuality. This piece is similar to aspects of text and tradition.

Finally, we act. We can assess what practice we should encourage, support, or choose. Action is absent from the quadrilateral but it is critical to liberation theology.

Here, two pieces are emphasized. First, I am not looking for the right rules (dogma). I am looking for better practices that will be reflected upon and lead to even better practices. Second, I begin by doubting all that has come before. Who said what? Why did they say it? For whose benefit? Then I turn to the experiences of people in the community.

I acknowledge this circle or spiral is messy. I try to separate out the pieces throughout this book simply to provide areas for further reflection. Working through the hermeneutical circle, we can assess our sexual poverty[4] and redress it.

What Other Academic Subjects Will I Include?

Liberation theologies encourage academic analysis of each situation. In particular, I consider global feminisms, intersectionality, and critical race theory. While feminism articulates how our society is patriarchal (male-dominated) and how society could shift toward equality for women, global feminism means thinking about women cannot be limited to white, US, middle-class women. An economically and socially just feminism recognizes that women are affected by injustice due to gender, economics, race, and so forth. With wealthier white men often making decisions, women are harmed and marginalized.

Often gender, race, and class are treated separately. However, such a separation is unhelpful as the overlaps nuance the discussion. Feminism needs to consider class, race, religion, and so forth because we do not exist in a vacuum. All is interconnected. We need to listen to the voices of a variety of women of color and poor women around the globe. People encounter both privilege and oppression, depending on their particular situations. One may be oppressed as a woman but privileged in her whiteness. One may be privileged in his wealth but oppressed due to his skin color. This is intersectionality. Privilege and oppression intersect in complicated ways that we will tease out as we address issues of sex.

With regard to race, critical race theory is important. As Europeans (whites) encountered people of different colors, "whites" tended to view "non-whites" as less than human. Hence, marriage between white and others was denigrated or banned, though people of color were often taken as sex slaves or mistresses by light-skinned men. Reproduction between the races was also frowned upon. During slavery, in the USA, for example, black slaves were to reproduce to provide further free labor for the masters. Yet, slaves could not marry. The male masters often had sex with the black slave women. After slavery ended, racism continued, as did the perceptions of black bodies as only for sex. Black women could be used by white men; black men were feared as it was assumed they would rape white women. This history lingers in the USA even today. Interracial marriage was only grudgingly allowed after a 1967 Supreme Court decision. Even today, interracial marriages only account for 14.5% of new marriages in the USA (Passel, Wang, and Taylor). Further, only 9% of whites marry outside their race.

Prioritizing men, heterosexuals, white people, enabling maltreatment of others affects each person negatively. How can we shift away from these notions? Throughout this book, I interrogate our assumptions about gender and sexuality. I have appended a list of definitions as a helpful guide. There is no separate chapter on gender and sexuality since I believe the notions pervade each of the issues I address. These concepts describe individual characteristics and notions constructed by our culture. So we can distinguish between how we identify as individuals and how society views us. Acknowledging all the possible spectrums both complicates our conversation and makes it more realistic.

Let us begin then with the hermeneutical circle to talk about sex.

See

As we begin to consider life-affirming relationships, we need to consider how the body has been denigrated and how power has negative effects on the body and sexual relationships, particularly through violence. Who gets to decide what good sex is and what bad sex is? This question will come up repeatedly in our conversation. Rather than think of normal/abnormal, I want us to think in terms of life-affirming.

Let's begin with the current situation around sex in the USA. While the average age a person begins to have sex is 17, the average age a person marries is about 26.[5] So half of teenagers have sex by 17, though many will not marry for at least 10 more years. If we think about the Christian tradition stating no sex before marriage, we see on average people experience at least ten years of sexual feelings and situations before they marry. For these ten years Christians are taught to deny all sexual feelings. Then, suddenly with marriage they can act upon them.

In addition, while many of us have had sex by age 17, many of us have also had unwanted sexual experiences. Four in ten women report being pressured into sex.[6] Clearly, we are not communicating well. There are gender-based assumptions and expectations at play here. First, heterosexuality is assumed and homosexuality has to be stated. Second, boys are expected to push for sexual access and girls are expected to resist. If we are not communicating well and base our interactions on gendered assumptions, we are probably not in healthy and life-affirming relationships.

In addition, sex brings us into intimate relations with another, intensifying the harm of bad communication and gendered expectations. We want intimacy and so open ourselves to danger. When we are intimate, we become vulnerable. Vulnerability is a key component of relationships. So the solution is not to remove vulnerability but to create safer spaces where we can be vulnerable.

Sex negativity within the Christian tradition may increase rather than decrease the possibility of harm. Sexual desire is deemed sinful. Christianity has focused on "thou shalt not" in terms of no sex except for within marriage for procreation, which excludes the majority of Christians around the world. I want to shift this frame.

Judge

Academics: The Body, Power, and Violence

How do we end up in harmful relationships? Here, I want to begin to unpack this harm in terms of the body, power, and violence. This analysis is a prior step to thinking through a positive sexual ethic.

All human beings have bodies. We communicate through our bodies, including through sexual intimacy. Thinking about our bodies as a part of sexual relationships is crucial. Christianity has often denigrated the body or ignored it, instead discussing the soul. However, this book emphasizes the body as a place for loving well. Bringing the body into the discussion is a first step.

Calling the body holy and sacred is a second step. The body in and of itself is important, created by God. The body should be supported, respected, and nourished. Understanding the body as a site of the sacred will inform our sexual ethics. As the New Testament tells us, God took on a human form in Jesus. Within this tradition, the human form is sacred.

Attention to the body is important in terms of gender, race, and ability. Women's bodies have been denigrated as less than men's; black bodies have been denigrated as less than white bodies. As Western history progressed, white Europeans and North Americans distinguished between civilized and uncivilized people. Civilized people could control their bodies: rationally and intentionally. In contrast, uncivilized people could not control their "animal" instincts. Sexual desire was placed in the "animal" realm. The female body, the black body, and the disabled body were considered uncivilized and out of control. I counter this narrative throughout the book while showing how it damages our understanding of desire and sex.

Next, I address the issue of power. First, we should each have the power to decide what to do with our bodies. Each person should have the right to say who can and cannot interact with them sexually. Sexual interactions must be between consenting individuals. This means individuals must (1) be able to consent and (2) have consented. However, power dynamics between individuals and in society make this two-part concept blurry. No one owns my body except for God. Even when I share my body with another in sex, it belongs to God, and no one else.

Power is often expressed as "power over." However, domination or coercing others is only one form of power. There is also "power to," empowerment. Empowerment is the power to act, to make choices.[7] Further, this type of power encourages sharing. When we empower each other, we both gain power. It is not a zero-sum game. I do not have to exercise my power over another to have power.[8]

Power is exercised in community. As many scholars have noted, power is about relations between people. These relations can be of dominance or of sharing and encouraging others to act. Further, power as dominance relies on hiding much of itself, being unspoken. This hiddenness enables us to be dominated without often noticing. We will unpack the concept of power to show how those with power have dominated the narrative around sex and desire, often without explicit statements. This understanding will enable us to resist the dominance and move toward a different exercise of power.

In sexual relations, "power over" is the more common understanding, particularly in heterosexual relationships. Men are expected to push and women submit. One is assumed to dominate the other in sex. Further, this domination is exacerbated by race, class, ability, and so forth. This domination and inequality can exist in many realms.

In particular, we need to think through the definition of "masculine." For many of us, to be masculine means superiority, in action, power, and intelligence. Yet, the definition of masculine is not fixed. It differs between cultures. Often, the notion of male as superior is accepted or remains hidden within our culture. Who do we see as a "real man?" Usually, the one in control, dominant. Men are dominant in society and this dominance spills over to sexual relationships. As noted earlier, many youth assume boys are supposed to push for sex and girls are supposed to resist. Masculinity does not have to mean dominance. Each person could be tender, kind, and giving. In our current culture, men enact their masculinity both against women (against femininity) and to show they are really men, as an identity of violence. Dominance is based on the tradition that the male protects the family, provides for the family, and has sex to reproduce the family. None of these statements needs be true.

Further, the traditional view of marriage where the woman takes the man's last name and promises to obey also assumes male superiority. The woman's own identity is subsumed into the man's; think about the language of two becoming one. Yet this one is not the woman. When two become one in marriage, the woman is subsumed under the man. This union creates an unequal power dynamic both between individuals and within society.

So how can we take these aspects seriously, counter them, and have a sexual relationship without this dynamic? First, in a heterosexual relationship, we can recognize and work to counter the assumed "power over" that rests with the man. (This dynamic may also exist in homosexual relationships, as one partner may dominate the other.) In any relationship, one person should not dominate the other. Even when an individual relationship may work to counter its internal power dynamic, the overlying structures must also be addressed. While I will address the importance of mutuality in relationships, it is always in the context of overturning the structural imbalances of power that exist. We emphasized power relations due to sex and gender here; however, those of heterosexuality, ability, race, nationality, religion, and so forth all contribute to the discussion throughout the book.

This individual and societal imbalance of power often leads to violence, particularly violence against women. Violence is inherent in our language about sex: bang, drill, nail, screw, hit, and so forth. Even the word "fuck" comes from the German word "to strike." Of the few nonviolent terms, "making love" is often seen as silly and few other options exist. Language, however, is not the only place of violence.

Violence is most clearly enacted in events of abuse and rape. However, while these are extremely negative actions, they are simply an extension of the support for male dominance. If men are to push and women are to resist, when does it become rape? Rather than view rape as an aberration, it can be viewed as an extreme example of the domination of one by another. In this case, the rape by a man is part of the larger gender hierarchy and notions around masculinity. In the words of one rapist, "rape gave me the power to do what I wanted without feeling I had to please a partner" (qtd. in Ellison 2012, 83). Rape is a clear example of power over, based on male dominance.

Male rapists may justify their behavior based on the wider culture of male dominance. They may argue that there are no rape victims because men are supposed to persist and women are supposed to resist. Abusers in general exert control over another person, forcing the person to comply with the abuser's wishes. Abusers use "power over" to attain what they feel is their rightful status. This is "rape culture."

The normalization of violence, linked to the broader culture of male violence and assumed heterosexuality, means women are often the victims. This victimization occurs in the most intimate of relationships. Home is not a safe space for women, although it has traditionally been considered a woman's space. Home is even more dangerous than a badly lit street at night. This fact poses a difficult paradox for women. In the search for an intimate heterosexual relationship, she places herself in danger. Is it possible to have a healthy sexual relationship within this nexus of power and domination?

In response to this recognition of the denigration of the body, of individual and structural imbalances of power, and that the notion of power as "power over" leads to individual and structural violence, what can be done? It is wrong to use power over another. Some ethicists argue that one should only enter a sexual relationship with another when there is mutuality and when the other person is of a similar class, race, religion, and other type of status. Could we create a micro-space of safety? How could these individual efforts engage the larger structures of power? They can be segregationist in varying ways. If I as a white middle-class able-bodied woman am limited to relationships with other white middle-class able-bodied women, if I am seeking relational justice, how would my relationship help the wider society?

The medical oath begins with "first do no harm." Our relationships could begin with this oath too. How would our relationships change if we did so?

Dealing with the Bible

Within the Christian tradition, the Bible is often the first source people turn to in order to understand how to behave. Unfortunately, it doesn't often clearly tell us. How can we read it? What does it include or exclude? Reading the Bible is far more complex than it appears because we first have to unpack the writing and reading of the canon we term the Bible. A document produced by men, addressed to men in a long ago patriarchal context, and interpreted by men throughout history requires a careful reading. I suggest we dive in with a true "hermeneutic of suspicion," subjecting everything we think we know to questioning.

The Bible does not always reflect the themes we want to interrogate. Yet, we try to read the Bible to analyze today's situation. We want to assess what should and should not be part of our sex and sexuality, what justice looks like, and so on. Was Mary, the mother of Jesus, a young woman forced by God to have a child and remained a virgin forever? Was she raped? Or did she shout from the rooftops: "I got to have sex with God!!!!" We do not know anything about Mary's sexuality, Jesus' sexuality, or God's sexuality.

While I will discuss some texts within the chapters, I want to give a brief summary now of a few pieces: (1) the historical context to some of the writings around sex and partnership; (2) examples of texts people often find surprising; and (3) a reminder of the distance between us and the writers of the text.

A Little History

During the centuries in which the Torah was formed, Jewish men tended to marry early, no later than age 20. Men had sexual access to their wives (there could be several) and their slaves. Women were subject to the desires of men, for example, Abraham's sex with Hagar in Genesis 16. In addition, wives brought dowries with them into marriage, encouraging multiple marriages by men. Marriage was the basis for procreation and continuation of the male lineage.

By the time we get to the New Testament in the first century C.E., the situation has shifted. First, the culture shifted to marriage between one man and one woman, though one might still marry more than once in a lifetime. Marriage tended to be later for men, after they could provide for a household. While men married around age 30, their wives were about 15–20 years old. A father needed to marry off a female before she got pregnant out of wedlock. We see here the decision-making still lay with men and marriage still ensured male lineage.

While marriages did last a lifetime, that lifetime was short. Life expectancy was only around 30 years of age, so men and women were married only for a short time.[9] While many died as children, few lived beyond age 50. Men and women were rarely married for more than 20 years. In addition, the man and woman could be at very different stages of life. A man might marry again after a first wife died, with him in his 40s and her 15, and so forth. The possibilities for marriage and family life were diverse though marriage was still for procreation.

Further, Jesus, Paul, and others valued celibacy more highly than marriage, so people would focus on spiritual practices. However, celibacy was not for everyone. Women were seen as weaker in controlling their desires, so Paul suggested marrying them if necessary. Paul hoped men would keep their sexual desire under control. However, if they could not, then marriage was the place to control desire. Divorce and marriage to more than one wife at a time were disallowed.

In summary, during biblical times (a long span), the onus for marriage remained with the man; the woman was assumed to fulfill the man's sexual desire and to provide children. Fathers had responsibility for ensuring the marriage of their daughters. Marriage ensured male lineage.

We also need to distinguish between what the text says about sex and sexuality and what historians know about the local situations. What is prohibited or allowed according to the text may not be what actually occurs. Further, what is prohibited or allowed was created by elite men, a situation that continues throughout Christian history.

Two Examples of Surprising Texts

There is a lot of sex throughout the Bible and varying sexual relationships are praised. I will provide just two examples here. The Bible has a complex view of desire, sex, partnership, the sex trade, and reproduction. Let's take the genealogy of Jesus as noted in Matthew 1. Here, the women listed are Tamar, Rahab, Ruth, Bathsheba, and Mary; see verses 1–16. Tamar prostituted herself to Judah, her father-in-law (Genesis 38). Rahab, a prostitute, gives birth to Boaz, David's great-grandfather (Joshua 2, 6: 22–25). Ruth seduced Boaz to get him to marry her. She gave birth to Obed, David's grandfather (*Book of Ruth*). Bathsheba was married when she had sex with David; David then killed her husband. She later gave birth to Solomon (II Samuel 11–12). Mary was engaged to Joseph when she became pregnant with Jesus. Each woman, although outside the norm of marital relations, is highlighted as an ancestor of Jesus through the lineage of David.

Our second example is the Song of Songs, an explicit love poem. To take just three excerpts: "Your two breasts are like two fawns, like twins of a gazelle that feed among the lilies" (4:5); "His body is a figure of bright ivory overlaid with sapphires" (5:14); "Your stature is like that of a palm tree, and your bosom like its clusters. I resolve that I will climb the palm tree; I will grasp its branches. Let your breasts be like clusters of the grapevine, and the scent of your breath like apples" (7: 7–8). Solomon is traditionally thought to be the author of this Song. The sex and desire shared are not between a husband and a wife and sometimes not simply between a man and a woman. We can also see through this poem a clear link between sexual desire and our communion with the environment.

So what does this tell us about text, tradition, and history?

The Distance Between Us and the Text

William Loader,[10] a biblical scholar, argues that reading the Bible is like being on a plane looking down at the land, mostly covered by cloud. The Biblical text does not tell us everything and it emerged within a particular context that is not fully understood. With regard to the actual having of sex, we know little.

Our context and culture is very different to that of the biblical texts. First, in many cultures today, marriages are not arranged by the parents of the future spouses. Instead, individuals choose a spouse. In addition, we usually do not subscribe to the same position of women in the culture. For example, we no longer tend to restrict women from speaking in church or require them to wear veils. While we still inhabit a patriarchal culture, some of the norms have shifted.

Also, we can now use contraception. In biblical times, early marriage was key for women to ensure children were born within the bounds of a marriage to carry on the paternal lineage. No one dated or waited to marry until they found a partner they loved.

Three further notions can be helpful. First, the biblical texts are not solely religious. They were meant to govern a community; thus the texts are political. They were written by powerful light-skinned men, mainly for powerful light-skinned men.

Women were seen to be inferior to men. At some points in biblical history, women were considered unformed or imperfect men, not even a separate sex. So here, we also note that the biblical text can be denigrating to women. Some refer to parts of the Bible as texts of terror, for example, women in the Book of Revelation. For women and other nondominant identities, these texts can be harmful.

Finally, we cannot look for a "rule" in the text. The text itself is complicated and the narrative is set within particular contexts and cultures. We may not want to base relationships on the notion of women as property, for example. We have to be aware of these complications when we read and acknowledge we will not find one rule to follow.

How, then, can we read? One possibility is to read the Bible through the lens of our desire for God and God's desire for humans.[11] The biblical text is a narrative put together by particular people for particular reasons. It focuses on the relationships between humans and God, God and the Hebrew people, and Jesus and humanity. In all of this, God desires relations with humans.

Liberation theology suggests reading through the lens of marginalized people and those excluded from our society. Search the text for ways to do justice. Search the text for ways to end harm.

Christian Tradition

This reading goes against the grain of much of the Christian tradition. Where the biblical texts appreciated sex within marriage for the purpose of procreation and its controlling of sexual desire, the early church moved further toward denigration of sex in general. As the church formalized its views on various issues, the early male theologians tended to value celibacy over all else. Secondarily, they approved of being married and celibate and then, thirdly, sex within marriage for procreation. Sex was not considered a way to know God; abstaining from sex was the ideal. Sex was considered sinful, unless within marriage for procreation. Sin meant violating one of God's laws; this violation required forgiveness through God's grace. One had to repent. We will rethink this understanding of sin as we move forward.

This understanding mirrored the denigration of the body. Such denigration came from the surrounding culture of the time and was absorbed by the early church theologians. For example, Plato, and others like the Stoics, began to address the soul and the body separately, prioritizing the mind and soul. These philosophies influenced early church theologians and Christians.

I will briefly present two such theologians here and throughout the book: Augustine[12] and Aquinas,[13] as their work is still influential today. Two of Augustine's works were titled *On Holy Virginity* and *On Marriage and Concupiscence*.[14] Augustine argued that with the sin of Adam and Eve in the garden, sexual desire came into being. From that point on, sin passed on to the children through sex. Hence, for Augustine, desire was sinful. While a married couple had to have sex to have children, sex still passed on sin. From the least to the most sinful sex, he advocates the following: sex for procreation is fine. Although he states that "abstention from all intercourse is better even than the marital intercourse that takes place for the sake of procreation" (Augustine, 76). Next, sex out of desire is forgivable if with a spouse, but only if one spouse if acting out of desire. "But if both partners are subject to such a desire (concupiscentia), they are doing something that clearly does not belong to marriage" (Augustine, 80). Further, sex with someone other than a spouse "carries a mortal fault" (Augustine, 76).

Sexual desire could not be positive or a way to know God because sexual desire came from sin itself. This understanding led Augustine to argue that husbands should "love in her [a wife] what is characteristic of a human being … hate what belongs to her as a wife" (Belliotti, 32). Women, as women, keep men from God. Women tempt men to sin. In slight contrast, Aquinas held the view that sexual desire was a part of sex before original sin. So we see an early church tradition that grudgingly admitted sex within marriage for procreation.

This negative perspective on sex and sexual desire persisted throughout Christian history. Within early forms of Protestantism, the main purposes of sex within marriage were to quell desire and to procreate. Within the Catholic Church, the same tradition continued. The Council of Trent stated that

> procreation and rendering the marriage debt are specified as the only morally legitimate motives for sex within marriage. … "The one who demands payment [translated, the man], who seeks sex for pleasure, or out of love … is guilty of sin, albeit a venial one [far less grave than mortal sin]. The partner who renders the debt [translated, the woman] is not in sin, for she … merely submits; she does not seek pleasure." (Belliotti, 41)

Here, the male is still in charge of the marriage. He can determine when the two will have sex. Second, the text assumes the male has the sinful desire; the female submits to male desire. Sexual desire is still sinful. Some aspects of the Christian tradition have acknowledged that sex can help the partners unite in marriage.

This sex-negative tradition has had damaging effects on all people. Nonheterosexual sex was considered even more sinful than heterosexual sex since there was no procreative possibility. In heterosexual relationships, women were given to men in marriage. Women were the property of men. Women gave birth to continue the male line. The contemporary tradition has not effectively countered these damaging assumptions or effects. For example, the Roman Catholic Church today still argues that sex is only allowed within a marriage between a male and female and must be open to procreation. Anything outside of this framework is sinful.

This negative tradition also contains racist elements. As maleness was seen as superior to femaleness in early Western history (and throughout), so too whiteness was considered superior to darker skin as Europeans came into contact with other races. The church understood its role to be to Christianize and civilize the darker races. Forced conversion went hand in hand with sexual subordination. After the end of slavery in the USA, whites in the USA attended lynching after Sunday service, still in their church clothes. Whites lynched black men, fearing those black men would harm white women. The same white men and women who sang praises to God inflicted vicious torture on black bodies, simply because they were black. Black meant uncontrollable sexuality; that sexuality had to be stifled to protect the white community. Still today in the USA, many churches are unofficially segregated and interracial relationships are not the norm.

Yet throughout Christian history, people have also worked against this grain, toward justice. Further chapters will tease out these counterpoints.

A Theology of Sex

From the theological perspective that sex can be a way to know God, Christian theology will be upended. I offer a few pieces for thought here that I will elaborate on throughout the book. First, as already implied, this is a theology of the everyday. We experience relationships with others in everyday life.

Second, we do theology in community. At its core, this theology is about relations between people in community. We come to know God through knowing others. We live with others, build lives with others. A Christian understanding of this community is communion. God created humans in communion with each other and God. Thus, theology happens in community.

Third, this theology views the body as a sacred site. Through our bodies, we relate to others and to God. The body is important, as even God became human in the person of Jesus. The notion of God becoming human means the body itself is important. Instead of devaluing the body, we value it. We value the body because it belongs to God. As God's body, it cannot be given away to another but the body can be shared. A healthy sexual ethic will enable each person to value their own body, accept it as good, including its desire for sex.

Fourth, this theology must reexamine the concept of sin. Sex and sexual desire are not sinful. Instead, the sin lies in the abuse of power. Rape is one clear example but so is any situation where one person exerts power over another. Exploitation rests on one person assuming another is less important, perhaps even less human. Our structures themselves sin as they exploit some people to benefit others. Once we move toward using another to benefit ourselves, we are on the slippery slope toward inhumanity. Further, we damage our relationship with God, since we come to know God through knowing others.

One cannot say that one sex act is good and another sex act is bad without knowing the context. Yet, the Christian tradition often does. Sex for procreation is good, for example. But what if one person is forcing another to have sex to have a child? Only recently did the courts (and much of the Christian tradition) recognize that rape can occur within marriage. The context in which our sexual relationships take place is key. For example, much of the intimate partner violence I have noted occurs within marriage. Throughout this book, I will name where abuses of power occur, rather than particular sex acts as good or bad. It is simply not true that sex within a marriage between a man and woman for procreation is good, while other sex is bad. While this traditional Christian rule may seem to make things straightforward, it hides a multitude of problems.

Fifth, this theology must unpack and work against the damaging structures of gendered inequality and the prioritization of heterosexuality. This work includes addressing the concept of masculinity itself. Masculinity should not be positively linked with domination and control. Instead, domination and control are negative for anyone. The notion of power over should be shifted toward "power to" or empowerment. Each person, regardless of sexuality, should be empowered to desire and love, individually and structurally.

Liberation theology aids us in this search for a healthy sexuality. The first liberationists did not consider sex or gender but their analysis applies to sexuality. Gustavo Gutierrez[15] argued that liberation was salvation. He defined salvation as communion between humans and between humans and God. This definition has implications for sex. Salvation includes communion between human beings sexually. Sin is when communion is broken, when injustice occurs, when power is misunderstood and misused. Sin is the absence of just relations.

Liberating Sex

To begin to liberate sex from its shackles, first, we must remember that sexual desire is good when directed toward knowing another, sharing power. The next chapter explains this statement further.

Next, in sexual relationships, play, humor, and feeling are important. Sex is to be enjoyed, laughed over. We need to learn to enjoy and celebrate sex, to share love with others. We can celebrate our bodies and pleasure.

Healthy sexual relationships build communion with God. We want to know God and so we long to know others, including sexually. According to scripture, what I do unto you, I do "unto Christ." So my sexual relationships are with Christ. Hence, rather than ask the question "what would Jesus do?" I ask "What would you do to Jesus?"—the fully human and divine Jesus Christ. Jesus is my sexual partner, the prostitute, the transgender person, the neighbor.

Healthy sexual relationships should be addressed between individuals and in terms of structures. First, as an individual, each of us should be educated on how to love and be loved in a sexual relationship. This education includes physical, emotional, intellectual, and spiritual components. We were made to commune with others and God and we need to learn how to do so well and justly. We long to relate intimately to others and we need education on how to relate well. This means we need sex education that includes everything from desire to sex to partnership. It also includes a frank discussion of power and empowerment. Sex education is more than thinking through where, when, and how one can have sex. We need to know how to develop relationships with others throughout the course of our lives. We need to think holistically about the self and the other/s.

In turn, preparing ourselves as individuals includes thinking of ourselves in community, in a network of relationships and institutions. This understanding of good relationships extends to the entire planet. We often miss this piece of the discussion.

The remainder of this book addresses these issues in detail: (1) Sexual Desire; (2) Having Sex; (3) Partnership; (4) Sex Work; (5) Reproduction.

Each chapter has the following plan:

(a) Definition of terms.
(b) Historical context: so we know a bit about why we tend to assume certain perspectives.

(c) Hermeneutical circle: (1) See; (2) Judge: Academics, Bible, Tradition, Theology; (3) Act.
(d) Moving forward: As all of this conversation is preliminary, to shift our thinking, I suggest how we might move forward in the conversation.

Questions for Reflection

I will include two to three questions for reflection at the end of each chapter. To begin:

1. What has your church or your family taught you about right and wrong with regard to sex?
2. To what extent do you agree with what you've been taught?
3. What, for you, would be three important characteristics of a "good" sexual relationship?

Further Suggested Readings

I will also list two to three further readings that would help you engage more deeply with the subject matter. Here I want to highlight three authors in particular.

For a good analysis of recent college student attitudes toward sex, see Freitas, Freitas, Donna. 2008. *Sex & the Soul: Juggling Sexuality, Spirituality, Romance, and Religion on America's College Campuses.* New York: Oxford University Press.

For a biblical analysis of sex and sexuality, see Knust, Jennifer Wright. 2011. *Unprotected Texts: The Bible's Surprising Contradictions about Sex and Desire.* New York: HarperOne and Loader, William. 2013. *Making Sense of Sex: Attitudes towards Sexuality in Early Jewish and Christian Literature.* Grand Rapids: Eerdmans.

Notes

1. Freitas writes and lectures on issues of sex, dating, and Christianity.
2. "The ecofeminist issue is born of the lack of municipal garbage collection, of the multiplication of rats, cockroaches, and mosquitoes, and of the sores on children's skin. This is true because it is usually women who have to deal with daily survival issues: keeping the house clean and feeding and washing children" (Gebara 1999, 2).

3. Known as the Wesleyan quadrilateral, see http://archives.umc.org/interior.asp?mid=258&GIC=312&GMOD=VWD
4. See the definitions listed in the appendix.
5. "A 2007 study documents that the median age of sexual initiation in the United States is 17 while the typical age for (heterosexual) marriage is 26 for women and 27 for men" (Ellison 2012, 119).
6. "A large number of youth (one in five males and four in ten females) reported unwanted sexual experiences, sometimes the result of physical force but often due to emotional pressure from their peers and their own desire for social acceptance" (Ellison 2012, 120).
7. "From this view, power is the ability or capacity to do things, that is, to achieve goals, make choices, and be self-determining" (Norsworthy et al., 62).
8. "Empowerment involves power sharing (Norwood & Zahau, in press); it is not based on the concept that when one person loses power, the other gains it, but instead is based on mutual enhancement (Miller and Cummins 1992)" (Norsworthy et al., 62).
9. William Loader notes: "Of women who lived beyond 15 more than half would die before they were 40 or perhaps even 35; many died in childbirth. It is estimated … that to end up with two children a woman would have to have given birth five times. For men life expectancy was *c.* 42–46" (Loader 2012, 102).
10. Loader is emeritus professor of The New Testament at Murdoch University in Perth, Australia.
11. See Jensen's book.
12. Augustine of Hippo lived from *c.* 354 to 430 CE. His writings strongly influenced the development of Roman Catholicism.
13. Thomas Aquinas lived from *c.* 1225 to 1274 CE. An Italian friar and priest, his work strongly influenced the Catholicism of his time and beyond.
14. His work is still argued over today, so I acknowledge this brief summary misses many of the details of his theology.
15. Gutierrez is a Peruvian priest and theologian, considered to be the "father" of Latin American liberation theology.

References

Augustine, St. 2002. From the Good of Marriage. In *Theology and Sexuality: Classic and Contemporary Readings*, ed. E. Rogers Jr., 71–86. Malden: Blackwell.

Belliotti, Raymond. 1993. *Good Sex: Perspectives on Sexual Ethics.* Lawrence: University Press of Kansas.

Ellison, Marvin. 2012. *Making Love Just: Sexual Ethics for Perplexing Times.* Minneapolis: Fortress Press.

Freitas, Donna. 2008. *Sex & the Soul: Juggling Sexuality, Spirituality, Romance, and Religion on America's College Campuses.* New York: Oxford University Press.

Gebara, Ivone. 1999. *Longing for Running Water: Ecofeminism and Liberation.* Minneapolis: Fortress Press.

Knust, Jennifer Wright. 2011. *Unprotected Texts: The Bible's Surprising Contradictions About Sex and Desire.* New York: HarperOne.

Loader, William. 2012. *The New Testament on Sexuality.* Grand Rapids: Eerdmans.

———. 2013. *Making Sense of Sex: Attitudes Towards Sexuality in Early Jewish and Christian Literature.* Grand Rapids: Eerdmans.

Norsworthy, K., M. McLaren, and L. Waterfield. 2012. Women's Power in Relationships: A Matter of Social Justice. In *Reproductive Justice: A Global Concern*, ed. J. Chrisler, 57–75. Denver: Praeger.

Passel, Jeffrey S., Wendy Wang, and Paul Taylor. *Marrying Out: One-in-Seven New U.S. Marriages Is Interracial or Interethnic.* Pew Research Center, June 4, 2010; rev. June 10, 2010. http://pewsocialtrends.org/files/2010/10/755-marrying-out.pdf

CHAPTER 2

Desire

Abstract This chapter analyzes and counters aspects of the Christian tradition that have tended to condemn sexual desire. Desire is part of God's creation of humans. Hence, desire is good. Desire is not a yearning for something lacking but an impetus toward being in relation. The goal is to cultivate desire in relation with others. Sexual desire is part of this overarching desire, which should be nourished and celebrated. Beginning with a new definition of desire, this chapter articulates a positive conception of desire through the Bible, tradition, and theology.

Keywords Desire • Eros • Body • Love • Communion

Our sexual desires begin early in life. They are confusingly both condemned as deviant and celebrated in the marketplace through our economic system. How can we overcome this tension? First, we need to understand the body as God's creation. Bodily desires are also God's creation. We will begin by defining desire.

We tend to negatively and incorrectly define desire. Desire is not a lack of something where possession is the goal. Desire is toward knowing; from a Christian perspective, toward knowing God. We tend to think desire can be satiated through acquisition but desire will not be satiated. Our desire comes from God. We desire to know God and to do so we need

T. Cooper, *A Christian Guide to Liberating Desire, Sex, Partnership, Work, and Reproduction*,
https://doi.org/10.1007/978-3-319-70896-6_2

to know others. We continue to desire, no matter what we have or who we know. Desire is inherently part of us. You cannot end desire.

This chapter begins with a positive understanding of desire, elaborated throughout. I then articulate how desire is integral to all relationships within a Christian perspective.

Definition

Dictionary.com defines desire as follows: "1. to wish or long for; crave; want. 2. to express a wish to obtain; ask for; request ... 3. a longing or craving, as for something that brings satisfaction or enjoyment ... 4. an expressed wish; request." These definitions make me anxious just thinking about them. What do I lack? How do I figure out what will satiate my desire? Who has ever satisfied their desire? Do I actually want my desire to end?

What would be a better definition? Here I make two shifts. First, desire does not signify a lack, but an impetus toward. Second, the goal is not to end desire but to deepen desire. Desire is the seeking to be in relation. Desire is the drive to be in relationship itself. Our desires grow in relation to another. We want to connect to each other and to God, a continuous productive desire, leading us to act. "Desire is love trying to happen" (Sebastian Moore quoted in Jensen, 34). This includes sexual desire.

Sexual desire "is a yearning for another person, a craving to unite with [sexually, I'd add] and to inspire the sexual desire of the other" (Belliotti,[1] 78). It is the drive and yearning to be in relation with another sexually.

This brings us to the question of love. Often we separate out friend love from erotic love. Friend love is seen as positive and erotic love as negative. I reject this perspective. I also reject the separation of love into various definitions. All are related rather than separate. Love is an emotion that wants good for others: love includes a sexual, intellectual, emotional, rational, physical component. Love inherently relates to justice.

Within the Christian tradition, desire is linked to eros (erotic love) and opposed to agape (disinterested love). Agape has been seen as positive, eros as negative and self-interested. Instead, eros can be seen as positive when desire is defined as this yearning for connection: the longing for all things good and beautiful according to Plato. This desire of eros is for the other, to build a relationship with another. We need to connect this eros to the proper definition of desire. Eros is a deeply relational love, sexual and sensual. Eros is loving another with our whole selves, fully being in relationship. Love for another because of the other, because we know God through knowing others. Our sexuality is part of the desire to know God.

Historical Context

Within the Jewish context, in the time of the Hebrew Bible, sexual desire was to be controlled through marriage, limited to one man and his wives and slaves. In New Testament times, the negativity surrounding sexual desire continued, contrasting itself with the surrounding culture. Throughout Western history, sexual desire has been the purview of men. As we will see, the Christian tradition condemns sexual desire but often places responsibility on the female to control men's desires. The woman is supposed to be without desire.

The attempt to control desire continued throughout our history. Within the USA, we banned certain expressions of sexual desire: homosexuality, interracial relationships, and so forth. The Puritans, for example, epitomized a Christian rejection of desire. More work needs to be done to unpack this historical understanding of desire as negative; it underlies our current reality.

This is not just about sexual desire but about desiring relation as a whole. With the onset of "rational" decision-making, as the height of civilization, the individual, rather than the community, became the focus. Individuals were assumed to be self-interested. The desire was to acquire for oneself. However, community and our desire for relations with others are not simply based on self-interest. Community is based on desire, love, and knowing.

The racial cast to the notion of sexual desire has also harmed many people. White men and women were seen as able to control their desire, while black people could not. White people associated the black body with uninhibited desire, seen as negative and dangerous. Black men were automatically considered suspect, even when simply near a white woman. Black women were also a danger to white men, as black women would attempt to seduce white men. We know, in contrast, that black women were subject to the sexual desires of white men, particularly under slavery. White people blamed black women for this subjection. Rather than being the seductress of common assumption, however, the black woman was mostly powerless against white male dominance.

This negative narrative created by white people led in many cases to a strict prohibition on desires within many black churches. If black people were going to be accused of being subject to sexual desire, in contrast, the churches taught them to be proper, to adhere to an even higher standard of behavior than white people. No white person should be able to make these statements. However, as we know, people often keep their stereotype's evidence.

To regain a positive notion of desire in all communities requires not only overturning a harmful sexual theology but also the harmful racism of white people, individually and structurally. It requires a two-step process: first, to see desire as holy and sacred again; and second, for those of us who are white, it requires us to understand that we perpetrated harm on communities of color when we classified them as "base" and to work to undo this harm.

Hermeneutical Circle

See

One of the main problems with our treatment of desire today is our connection of desire with possession, exclusive ownership of something. We tend to split desire into two areas: economics and sex. Economic desire is considered good. Seeing desire as an urge to be fulfilled by possession drives our market-based capitalist society. Capitalism teaches us our desires are unlimited, thus our yearning to purchase goods is unlimited. The only way to satiate economic desire is to purchase.

We consider sexual desire negative in part because we assume sexual desire is satiated through sex. So we want to "own" access to sex. For example, I want to know another person; knowing is wrongly connected to possession so if I know someone sexually, you cannot. Why do we think only one connection is allowed? I have this person I desired; now I should be satiated. However, desire cannot be satiated. Sexual relationships sometimes end because a participant expects their desires to be fulfilled and they are not. Desire, however, is not to be ended but cultivated. The following chapters consider this further through sex and partnership.

How might we need to overturn accepted notions of desire? For example, male desire to possess was seen as normal. Marriage and heterosexuality are two components that buttress and are buttressed by this. Power over and desire to possess meet in the patriarchal structures. Further, since the body is the seat of sexual desire, and throughout Christian history the body was subsumed under the soul, sexual desire was assumed to be negative. Instead, we need to think about it positively, an expression of our bodily selves.

Gilles Deleuze[2] claimed desire is productive, creating connections and relationships.[3] This understanding of desire is connected to the argument I made in the introduction that we tend to equate power with "power over" rather than "power to" or empowerment. We mistake and misuse desire when we try to attain the completion of desire. Desire cannot be sated; it continues.

Desire continues because it inherently wants to be in relation. Desire is a longing from God, for God and for others, to know others. Desire is the impetus to be in communion with others; God created this desire.

This desire exists in all realms, not just the sexual realm, though that is our focus in this book. This concept of desire as knowing and sharing, rather than possessing, would impact the economic realm, for example. What would an economic system look like focused on humans in a community, knowing each other? How might we distribute resources? How much would we accumulate for ourselves and why?

Further, desire as knowing and sharing, rather than possessing, would change the way we try to control desire, impacting the political realm, among others. Categorizing desire as an urge to possess would be simpler. Then it could be answered by marriage, a purchase, and so on. However, desire is far more complicated than this. This desire to know cannot be corralled into something simple. There are many people to know and many ways to know people. In the past, viewing desire as negative, we have been only allowed to fully know one person, of the opposite sex, within marriage. We see this difficulty emerge even within friendships. Friendships ebb and flow. There is often jealousy when one ebbs and another flows.

In our case, we will consider the concepts of friendship and partnership, sex work, and reproduction in the following chapters. If desire encourages knowing and sharing in abundance, not possession in scarcity, how should our systems change? How should we regulate desire and why?

Judge

Academics

In economics, we see desire has been assumed to be temporarily satiated through possessing the thing we desire. Once I purchase that new pair of shoes I will be briefly satiated. Once I have that lover, I will be briefly satiated. Hence, we tend to be possessive in relationships. Either I have a person or another does. Either I own the shoes or another does. If I desire another person, I want him/her to be my man or my woman, not someone else's. Yet, we each belong to God. We cannot belong to another human being. That is slavery, unjust and sinful.

Possession limits desire. This wrong-headed notion of desire leads to wrong-headed notions of sex and relationships that we unpack in the following chapters. Possession limits the relationships human beings have. Instead, desiring others could lead us to a more just world.

We also need to remove the patriarchal aspects prioritizing male desire over female desire. As we will see in the chapters on sex and marriage, throughout Western history, it was assumed that males desire and females give in to this desire. Even within marriage, the woman was to have sex with the man to keep him from straying outside the marriage. Two assumptions prevailed: first, the woman did not want to have sex; second, the woman should have sex anyway.

Further, eros, like desire, is about more than sex. Eros is any deep yearning: emotional, spiritual, and physical; it is at our core. Eros emphasizes connection; eros does not live in the individual alone. In ignoring this important part of love, we ignore our deepest selves and our ability to connect with others creatively, spiritually, and emotionally. Limiting eros to sexual desire constrains us too. Most of us were taught to hold our deepest desires in check, to limit them. In contrast, I want us to explore our eros, explore how sharing our deepest desires could deepen our relationships.

Understanding the connection between desire and eros can then help us think about our relationships in terms of the wholeness of life. If the yearning for connection is "one of the deepest principles for life" (Isherwood[4] 2008, 203), then our desire enables us to have relationships within society as a whole. If we celebrate rather than control desire, it can help us connect to each other. Rather than having rules of thou shalt not, we can follow our bodily, emotional, and other desires to work for good.

How would this shift happen? First, we need to see a link between sexual desire and justice in society. Our definition of desire does this. Desire is yearning for connection, sexual and otherwise. If we yearn to connect rather than to possess, desire would reorder our society, toward justice. Yes, this shift seems like a huge idea when all you want to know is how to have good sex. But this is good sex! Sexual desire can lead to justice.

Many sexual relationships, based on using our power to "get" and keep another, are unjust. We treat our bodies unjustly. We treat each other unjustly. If I have power over my partner, that is unjust. If I see that as normal, then why would I think other relationships, even wider societal structures, are unjust? We are used to this inequality. However, true desire and eros is to know another. Knowing another leads to wanting the other to flourish. Racism, classism, sexism, and unjust intimate relationships are all linked. Personal injustice and structural injustice are linked. At its base is a wrong-headed notion of desire.

Bible

We can read the Bible as a narrative of desire, rather than as critical of desire. This reading includes God desiring us, us desiring God, and us desiring each other. This desire expands throughout scripture. God desires communion with humans and forms a covenant with humans in the Hebrew Bible. In the New Testament, God sends Jesus into the world, God becoming human. Here too, God forms a covenant with humanity.

Let's take the Hebrew Bible as an example. In Genesis, 2:23, Adam expresses an aspect of desire: "This at last is bone of my bones and flesh of my flesh." Still, the example is tainted as we do not hear Eve's perspective and this desire is possessive. The text offers further examples of where desire can mutate into possession, rather than sharing and delighting in one another, for example, the desire to possess the fruit. Having it present is not enough. When Adam and Eve do possess it, desire is not satiated. Instead, they become embarrassed and are punished by God (Genesis 3: 16–17). In contrast, desire is about sharing in abundance.

In the main, the desire expressed in the Bible is of men. However, Song of Songs is an exception. Here, we hear a woman's voice; she is not acting in concert with societal expectations. She is in love and desires her lover. Many writers have considered what this text means in the Jewish and Christian contexts. She clearly expresses and celebrates her desire.

Some within the Christian tradition argue that this text is an extended metaphor of God's love for the church. Yes, God desires as well. If the text is talking about God's love for the church, it does so in clear comparison with sexual desire, the desire for physical, emotional, intellectual, and spiritual connection.

Reading the Song can upend our notion of "proper sexual desire." The desire is explicit and does not follow societal rules. In chapter 3: 1–3, the woman goes after her lover rather than waiting for him to come to her. Then she brings him to her home. The woman is in charge of her own desire. This desire is not ordered by society. It is free and open.

Though the Christian tradition has often assumed the New Testament to be against sexual desire, one can read these texts differently too. To take one scholarly debate, while some argue Paul wanted to end sexual desire, others argue Paul simply critiqued excess desire.[5] So the contrast here is whether all desire is bad or whether uncontrolled desire is bad. In both cases, however, desire is to be suppressed.

In contrast, I argue that we should celebrate desire because desire is the drive to be in relation rather than to possess.

Christian Tradition

Traditionally, the Christian churches portrayed sexual desire negatively. For example, Augustine saw sexual desire as something that came after the sin in the Garden of Eden. Before this event, Augustine argued, sex was solely for procreation, without desire. One could decide to have sex rationally, without emotion, to produce a child. After the original sin, sexual desire reared its ugly head; Augustine saw his erection at the sight of a woman as negative, something to be tamed. To give in to desire was sinful. While desire was a sin for both men and women, within the patriarchal context, the woman was responsible for controlling her desire as well as any man's.

Within the Christian tradition, Eve was often blamed for original sin. This blame extended to women in general. In this view, Eve sinned by eating the fruit AND by tempting Adam to do so. She used her sexual desire to tempt him. Hence, women were seen as dangerous to men. Women were the source of sin and the source of the temptation for men to sin. This condemning of women as temptresses continued within marriage. Augustine compared loving a wife with loving one's enemies. The early church theologians saw the woman's body as sinful and a site of sin.

While the majority of the tradition condemned desire, some within it have tried to reinterpret desire. For example, Bernard of Clairvaux[6] argued that humans feel desire because they were created to move toward a goal: knowing God. Thus, desire is positive, a gift from God. God desires us. We desire each other and we desire God. This desire is connected to love: love for others and love for God. Desire makes us want to do things for each other, to know each other.

Further, the Trinity shows that God is in relation and can be used as a model for our relation. God, Jesus Christ, and the Holy Spirit are all in close communion with each other, part of each other. More work needs to be done on this concept as well. The desire for relation can bring us into communion, community. Sexual desire is part of this overarching desire.

Theology

So what is healthy sexual desire?

1. God created us to desire. God desires us and enables us to desire each other and God. This includes sexual desire. We cannot possess what we desire; we can only know it. If we mistake desire for an urge to possess, then we are no longer working with eros. Here, sin enters the equation. When desire turns toward possession, idolatry emerges. One worships something other than God. The other is to be desired FOR the other, to know God, not for ourselves. Because we assume desire is the urge to acquire, because it is not satiated when we "have," we assume it is because we "have" the wrong thing and move on to something else. Instead, we need to realize that desire cannot be sated because we cannot fully know another or fully know God. God is infinite and humans are finite. We will continually desire to know others and to know God and that desire is positive; it helps us to develop our own eros and to empower others. Desire errs when it aims to possess.
2. This desire is to know others and share with others in fullness, abundance. Hence, it is not exercising power over but sharing. Despite humans constantly linking desire to possession, God continues to advocate abundance. Throughout the biblical text, we see God recommitting to humans despite our stubbornness over possession. God creates and recreates the covenant with the Israelites despite their actions, and in the New Testament, God also sends Jesus in another show of commitment. The notion of desire in abundance and sharing rather than scarcity and possession is also present in other religious traditions. True desire can be shared with others. We desire the fullness of life; we desire others. This desire comes from the urge to know God, a fullness, rather than an emptiness. God created us out of abundance; we desire to share in this abundance with others. We live out desire in community; we can see this in the Trinity. In the Trinity, three are one and each one is part of the three. Each piece is complete in itself and is also fulfilled in the others. They exist in such close relation to each other that the three are one. Nothing is lacking in God, Jesus, or the Holy Spirit but they are also fulfilled together.
3. This desire cannot be satiated; it continues and grows. Desire comes from God and is fulfilled in God through knowing others. In fact, we can desire many others, contrary to what the Christian tradition has taught us about relationships. Because desire moves from fullness to

fullness, it is possible to love the world, each other, and God. Sexual desire is for God and others, to live in fullness. It is about being in relation with another human, deep relation, communion. Joining in sex with another can build desire, to keep knowing the other. True desire does not wane over time. One cannot fully know another just as one cannot fully know God. Sex can be a way to come to know another and this knowing can deepen over time. This desire requires each person in communion to want to know the other. We need not limit desire to one person as I will address in the partnership chapter.

4. We should cultivate desire rather than suppress it. One way is through sexual relations. Structures should cultivate desire too. The following chapters consider this.
5. Healthy sexual desire can lead to justice. Again, the following chapters will consider this concept. However, celebrating sexual desire as a gift from God can help us work to end racism, sexism, classism, and so forth. Celebrating sexual desire not only removes the negativity around desire itself but also removes the negativity we placed on women, people of color, the poor, and people of varying sexualities, all of whom we deemed throughout history to be subject to desire and thus less civilized.

Act

1. Redefine desire. Use the new definition. Talk about it with others. Focusing on desire as yearning for connection rather than possession can upend our relationships and structures.
2. Celebrate desire. Share your desires with others. Talk about your eros.
3. Use desire to change the world for good. We connect to the world through our senses. Desire gives us the yearning to use these senses to know others in the world. If we channel this desire to know, rather than to possess, it can change our sexual relationships and the world beyond. From within the Christian tradition, we can see desire as positive. Desire, including sexual desire, motivates us to live in relation with others, all others. We will consider racism, sexism, and so forth in later chapters; however, understanding desire as this God-given yearning for connection can motivate us to work for the good of others, all others.
4. Cultivate desire. Our ethics of relationships can stem from this desire for connection. Once we know we yearn for connection, we can trust our desire. We can think about how desire can lead us toward good. We tend to disparage our desire. Instead, we should cultivate and celebrate desire.

Moving Forward

So how can desiring help us?

First, let us remember the body is sacred. Celebrate and cultivate bodily desires.

Second, desire is a good that helps us to relate to each other and to God. Using this understanding, we will consider sex and sexual relationships.

Finally, we can consider that desire is not "to have sex" but desire can lead to sex. Desire is not to possess something we lack, but to be in relation itself, including sexual relations.

Questions for Reflection

1. How would you now define desire?
2. How might an understanding of desire as relational rather than possessive affect a sexual relationship?
3. Write down one way you could cultivate desire rather than repressing it.

Further Suggested Readings

Jensen, David. 2013a. *God, Desire, and a Theology of Human Sexuality.* Louisville: Westminster John Knox Press.

Jensen's book works through theological concepts of scripture, God, Christ, Eschatology, Holy Communion, vocation, and finally ethics to articulate a Christian theology of desire. Arguing that desire is important theologically to people of faith, he leads the reader through complex theological topics clearly and concisely to a better understanding of desire and sex from a Christian perspective.

Lorde, Audre. 2010a. "Uses of the Erotic: The Erotic as Power." In *Sexuality and the Sacred*, eds. Marvin Ellison and Kelly Brown Douglas, 73–77. Louisville: Westminster John Knox Press.

Lorde's classic essay counters the rejection of eros by the Christian tradition. Instead, she considers eros as a source of power, particularly for women. Eros can be empowering and creative.

Thatcher, Adrian. 2011a. "Desiring." In *God, Sex, and Gender: An Introduction.* Malden: Wiley-Blackwell, 57–75.

Thatcher's fourth chapter focuses on "Desiring." He considers desire in light of the concept of lust, as well as the varying assumptions we make about what desire is. He concludes by articulating how we desire God and how God desires us.

Notes

1. Raymond Belliotti is the Distinguished Teaching Professor of Philosophy at SUNY Fredonia.
2. Deleuze was a French philosopher who lived from 1925 to 1995.
3. Daniel Bell, Jr., a professor and ethicist, explains Deleuze's understanding of desire: "Desire produces; it gives. It works. It creates. Desire is a positive force, an aleatory movement that neither destroys nor consumes but endlessly creates new connections with others, embraces difference and fosters a proliferation of relations between fluxes of desire" (Bell, 44).
4. Lisa Isherwood is Professor of Feminist Liberation Theologies and the Director of the Institute for Theological Partnerships at the University of Winchester, UK.
5. "Dale Martin argues that Paul believed that the truly fulfilled human life is one in which all sexual desire is simply extinguished. … Will Deming counters this argument by noting that, for Paul, the goal was not the *absence* of desire but the ability to restrain an *excess* of desire – a problem addressed in other Stoic literature" (Brownson, 138).
6. Bernard was a French abbot who lived from 1090 to 1153 CE.

References

Bell, Daniel. 2012. *The Economy of Desire: Christianity and Capitalism in a Postmodern World*. Grand Rapids: Baker Academic.

Belliotti, Raymond. 1993. *Good Sex: Perspectives on Sexual Ethics*. Lawrence: University Press of Kansas.

Brownson, James. 2013. *Bible, Gender, Sexuality: Reframing the Church's Debate on Same-Sex Relationships*. Grand Rapids: William B. Eerdmans.

Isherwood, Lisa. 2008. Will You Slim for Him or Bake Cakes for the Queen of Heaven? In *Controversies in Body Theology*, ed. Marcella Althaus-Reid and Lisa Isherwood, 174–206. London: SCM Press.

Jensen, David. 2013. *God, Desire, and a Theology of Human Sexuality*. Louisville: Westminster John Knox Press.

Lorde, Audre. 2010. Uses of the Erotic: The Erotic as Power. In *Sexuality and the Sacred*, ed. Marvin Ellison and Kelly Brown Douglas, 73–77. Louisville: Westminster John Knox Press.

Thatcher, Adrian. 2011. Desiring. In *God, Sex, and Gender: An Introduction*, 57–75. Malden: Wiley-Blackwell.

CHAPTER 3

Sex

Abstract This chapter analyzes and counters the Christian tradition's tendency to disparage sex. Sex should not be limited to within marriage for procreation. Sex can be a way to know God. Beginning with the understanding of sexual desire as an impetus to be in relation, good sex involves play, communion, and the holy, bringing us into closer relation with each other and God. Beginning with a definition of "having sex," this chapter explores the sex-negative historical context and articulates how to have good sex with reference to the biblical tradition, the Christian tradition, and theology.

Keywords Sex • Desire • Orgasm • Communion • Power • Mutuality

Having redefined desire as an impetus to be in relation, let's talk about sex. Sex is rarely discussed in the same breath as God. But I am a theologian and I am sexual. So why pretend I'm not? If we want to figure out how to have ethical sexual relationships, we need to talk about sex.

The Christian tradition limited sex to within a marriage between a man and a woman for procreation. Men sat atop the hierarchy, entitled to possess women. Within this possession, good sex was to procreate, bad was from desire. Even within marriage the male took priority over the female. All desire was to be repressed until the marital bed, where the male's desire then took precedence.

T. Cooper, *A Christian Guide to Liberating Desire, Sex, Partnership, Work, and Reproduction*,
https://doi.org/10.1007/978-3-319-70896-6_3

Within marriage, there is still no teaching on good sex. Within the Christian tradition, we are taught to get married and then have sex. Our desires can suddenly be fulfilled without any education. In contrast, this chapter talks about what good sex looks like. Even if one did limit sex to within marriage for procreation, we should still learn what good sex is. I reject the limiting to marriage and procreation, as later chapters will argue. Here, I offer starting points for how we can talk about just sex. It is difficult to imagine that we come to know God through knowing others and that sex can be a way to know God.

Good sex is enjoyable, fair to the parties involved, and good for the community at large. How can Christians have liberating sex? Sex can be an exchange of love, a knowing, that leads us to God. "Sex is an art form, a prayer, a way of contemplating and communing with infinite love, naked, unafraid, raw and totally open" (Deida[1] 2002, 3–4). Sex can be a form of worship. Humans are finite and God is infinite. Hence I come to know God through developing relationships with other humans, to build a fuller picture of God. What would just sex look like without racism, classism, heterosexism, and so on? Sex is a bodily and emotional way to express love. Sex is an extension of our desire to know others. Loving others through sex is a way to know God.

To have liberating sex, we need to remember the body is positive, address issues of power, and reject violence. Sex and desire are positive aspects of bodily knowing, when shared mutually. This chapter seeks to overturn the negativity and offer a sexual ethic for justice.

Definition

First, we have to define "having sex." I can attest to the fact that even after hours of discussion in my classroom, students rarely agree on a definition of "to have sex," never mind what good sex might be.

Intercourse: Intercourse itself involves penetrative sex. To have sex includes far more than intercourse.

To have sex: former President Bill Clinton's definition of sexual relations was contact with a person's genitalia to gratify sexual desire. In this way, Monica Lewinsky was having oral sex when she fellated Clinton; however, he was not having sex. Here, female to male oral sex, though it gratifies the man, is not sex for the man but it is for the woman. This distinction is flawed, though many women may agree that sex does not often gratify the woman.

Sex is intimate contact with another person, encompassing a broad range of possibilities. A definition should include vaginal intercourse, oral sex, genital touching, exploring a partner's naked body, having an orgasm with another person, anal intercourse, and so forth. People also sometimes need a third party to help them engage in sex. Often, our attempt to limit the definition of "having sex" is due to a notion of preserving virginity. Some women, for example, exclude anal intercourse from the definition of "having sex." They have anal intercourse but refrain from vaginal intercourse, remaining "virgins." Rather than finding a technical definition to constrain sexual activity, I will be inclusive in this chapter, as I articulate how to have good sex.

Further, sex is not limited to one act. It is a process.

Historical Context

Within the Western tradition, sex without the possibility of procreation was condemned and often banned by law. As the previous chapter explained, sexual desire was negative, controlled by marriage. Sex was allowed within narrow conditions. For the early Jewish population, procreation was critical and men had many wives and slaves in order to ensure the male lineage through sex.

Michel Foucault[2] distinguished two approaches to sex in history: one teaches sex as an erotic art and one does not, the Western Christian tradition in particular. China, Japan, India, the Roman empire, Greece, and Arab countries all have teachings on pleasure. Pleasure can be positive, a way to improve the body and soul. Sex can serve as a means of learning and transmitting knowledge. This understanding leads to a different assessment of good sex. For example, people often reflect on the positive approach to homosexuality in ancient Greek society. Yet, this assessment is incomplete. The desire for the beautiful was positive. Foucault notes that any body could be considered beautiful. This encompassed male–male relations. The key was for the adult male to remain dominant; hence, younger men could have sex with older men but when the younger men reached a certain age this submission became questionable.

The Jewish and Christian traditions, however, did not think about sex as a means of teaching the erotic. In the Jewish context of the first century, sex remained suspect but allowed within marriage for procreation. Sexual desire was seen as needing to be controlled, with a variety of laws to this effect. This combination persisted into the Christian tradition.

Medically, women and men were considered one sex, though men were the perfect version and women the imperfect. Galen[3] (*c.* 129–216 CE), for example, stated that men had genitals on the outside and women on the inside. Sperm from both created a fetus. It was thought that women needed to achieve orgasm too to release their sperm. When this notion was later overturned by biological science, the focus on the woman's pleasure in sex diminished.

Further, any exceptions within the Christian tradition for sex outside of marriage were given to the male. For example, soldiers could have sex with prostitutes or native women but not masturbate or have sex with another man. The urge for sex was somewhat natural and if the marital bed was unavailable, sex should still be with a woman.

Christianity has taken a law-based approach to sex. When laws are broken, Christians must confess and repent. So here, sex was both negative and an obsession. While most sex was prohibited, the continuous confession of sins kept it at the forefront of the mind, which I will discuss further in the tradition section.

In the eighteenth century, this negative tradition took on a medical, scientific cast. Foucault identifies four areas of focus: "the hysterical woman, the masturbating child, the Malthusian couple, and the perverse adult" (Foucault I, 105). These areas are critical to our understanding of what sex is considered negative and why. Almost all illness and violence was attributed to sex. Children masturbating, darker races reproducing, women's illnesses, all had to do with sex. This sex must be prohibited. Hence, again we see an obsession with sex, though the sex is negative.

First, sexual desire was considered inherent to women's bodies. This desire was negative and pathological. Female sexuality needed to be controlled for society to function.

Second, children were curious about their own bodies. However, any masturbation was negative. Masturbation was both a natural curiosity and a wrong. Children had to be kept from sexuality.

Third, there was a focus on procreation: procreation for the correct type of people. Couples were responsible either for procreating or, if they were from "uncivilized" groups, not to procreate. Healthy, wealthy whites should procreate; others should not.

Finally, there was a focus on "perversity." No longer did a person simply commit a perverse act. This perversion was inherent to the person. The person was perverse himself or herself. This perversion had to be corrected.

This shift to medicalization was also a shift from thinking about a person acting in a certain way to a person BEING a certain way. A person no longer simply committed a homosexual act; that person was a homosexual. A child did not simply masturbate; that child was a masturbator. Thinking shifted from a person going against a law of nature to the person being perverse. A white heterosexual marriage aimed at procreation was normal. Anything else regarding sex was not.

To take one example here of the trend toward fixing sexual perversities, women were sometimes prescribed orgasms. This prescription may seem odd to us now; however, one way to control a "hysterical" woman was to ensure she had regular orgasms. Doctors manipulated women to orgasm with their hands, jets of water, and through vibrators. The first battery-operated vibrator was invented in 1880 by a doctor. Resorts marketed their various vibrating equipment for the "healing" of women. In my favorite note on this subject, the Hamilton Beach company patented an electric model. It was the "fifth electrified domestic appliance after the sewing machine, the fan, the teakettle, and the toaster, and preceded the vacuum cleaner and iron by a decade" (Abbott, 115). While female orgasm can be a positive aspect of sex, orgasm as an enforced treatment to "heal" ill women to bring them back into a functioning society is not.

Further, racism is important to consider here too. In Southern USA, under slavery, many white men had their first sexual experience with a slave. Black people were assumed to be more animalistic and thus to have uncontrollable sexual desires. In response, some black Christians repressed their sexuality. So in terms of race, I need to think about how I, as the descendant of white people, harmed others by critiquing sex and to understand how to celebrate sex as a way to know God.

White men killed black men because white men assumed black men were out to rape white women. This notion is patriarchal and racial. First, we know men are supposed to desire women and women are to stop men from acting on those desires. Within the white community this is constrained by marriage. White culture saw black people as less able to control their sexual desire. Thus, black men were out to have sex with white women. Black male desires were so uncontrollable that white men had to protect "their" women. Hence, white men killed any black men they suspected of interacting with a white woman, even saying hello, because it was assumed to be a prelude to sex.

Some black Christians, then, downplayed their sexuality. This led to a rejection of homosexuality, in particular. In trying to overturn the white stereotype, some black Christians denied any link to a perception of sexuality. Black Christians were good Christians, solely having sex for procreation within heterosexual marriages. Anything else was rejected because it would lead to further denigration in the white culture's eyes. The eros we discussed in the previous chapter could not be part of the spectrum of a black Christian society because of white racism.

If you are a white person reading this book, you may wonder why we are discussing race in a book about sex. Our society's predilection for circumscribing sex for particular people in particular ways is racist, ablest, sexist, and so forth. Sometimes, as part of the "privileged" portion of society, we never think about injustice, because it benefits us. However, notions around sex were constructed over our cultural history as animalistic, negative, and have often been experienced through violence.

Hermeneutical Circle

See

Several of the historical problems I noted around the issue of sex continue today. First of all, the definition of having sex often excludes many people, whether homosexual, transgender, disabled, and so forth. Laws continue to proscribe certain sexual interactions. In some countries, homosexual sex is still banned. Interracial sex was banned in many places until recently.

Second, we have no education on good sex. We are not taught how to please ourselves and our lovers. We are not taught how to deal with the emotions involved.

Third, many cultures still prioritize men and male desire. Heterosexual sex is often considered completed when the male orgasms. Any non-male desire is dismissed. Women often internalize this dismissal. For example, one study reported 26% of women do not regularly have orgasms, 32% state they are not interested in sex, and 23% state sex is not pleasurable (Rubio, 243). Further, many women stated they did not masturbate in their teenage years, considering masturbation as wrong. Yet, how can we learn about sex if we cannot experiment with ourselves to see what we find pleasurable?

Fourth, we often think about how regularly we have sex as the measure of a relationship, but we rarely pay attention to the quality of that sex. Is the sex good for all involved? Sex is more than "wham, bam, thank you ma'am"; sex is about the process of intimacy with another human being.

A healthy sexual relationship involves both partners sharing in the pleasure and care for one another, physically, mentally, emotionally, and intellectually. This sharing and caring has not been the focus. In our culture, we tend to "hook up." We have sex before dating and sex with no dating at all. We need to consider what these experiences mean. How do they feed us emotionally? While "hooking up" is not inherently negative, we should explore why we want sexual experiences without any features of friendship. How can we craft a level of trust with another person to have good sex?

A Brief Example of Good Sex

What would it look like to cum to know God? How many of you have heard of a cervical orgasm? A feeling different to other orgasms, a cervical orgasm is often described as a religious, spiritual, emotional, and physical experience. In this orgasm, women report feeling beauty, happiness, expansion, and deep connection with their partner and beyond that can last hours, even days, after the event. Partners, even those without a cervix, report sensing the woman's openness, her peace, and a deep emotional, spiritual, and physical connection. As the cervix is stimulated and during the orgasm, intense emotions are felt: sadness, joy, and so forth. Often women will weep without quite knowing why.

This orgasm is more than a physical experience. When a partner touches the cervix for the first time, the cervix is often numb or painful. With patience, other sensations can be felt. To have this patience requires trust in the partner, to know the partner will stop when asked, continue when asked, and sense your mood changes and needs. It can take days or weeks of gentle touching before the cervix becomes sensitive and receptive to touch. This trust is crucial to achieve the orgasm, as there is a sense of expansion far beyond the body that can feel overwhelming. One must be able to cry and yell with the partner, be comforted, told she is loved and safe. To let yourself move beyond the physical into the emotional and spiritual realms, connecting with the world beyond you is risky.

Many women have never had a cervical orgasm. First of all, this fact is telling. How many people with a cervix have had sexual experiences where they would be comfortable enough to let go fully? Even clitoral and vaginal orgasms require some aspect of letting go. Orgasms can occur without physical contact but it is difficult to orgasm without sensual/emotional contact (even with yourself).

However, there is more to sex than an orgasm. Orgasms are lovely but so is the entire sexual process. Desire continues to grow. Orgasm can cultivate that desire but it is not the end or aim of desire. The desire is for connection in the process of sex.

Further, you can have a sexual connection with someone without ever touching them. Think about meeting someone's eyes across a room. Something sensual can occur simply with a look.

Sex is more than one act; it is the intimate experience of relation. This relation does not have to be spectacular at every moment but the process itself can be spectacular. Sex can be a normal everyday event, a habit, a process over time.

The goal of sex is to experience pleasure in connection with other human beings. It is not to ejaculate, to fall in love, to feel love. All of these things are lovely but if the sexual process is limited to any of these, it will fail. We will not always orgasm or feel love. However, sex is a way to grow in love, in relation to the world.

Right now I feel like a self-help book. You are reading and asking "yes, but how do I have great sex? It's nice to explain that it could exist. But frankly, it doesn't. Stop being gooey and speak." So let me move to analyzing the process of sex with academic tools.

Judge

Academics

Why don't we have great sex? Recent Western history shows us that the narrative of sex crafted by those in power has made sex the purview of men for procreation, predominantly. If you do not fit this category, you are either perverse or invisible or both. Power has inscribed permitted sex and prohibited sex.

Let's unpack some of the assumptions and effects of patriarchy relevant for sex. The man is considered superior to the woman and should protect her, even from her own sexuality. This patriarchal control system circumscribes the position of men, women, and transpeople. Regarding sex, two arguments predominate: (1) Women and men love sex. All women pretend they don't want sex but they do. The male's job is to convince the woman to have sex. Good women resist; bad women give in. (2) Women hate sex; men love sex. Men deserve sex; women can be coerced. The male's job is to coerce the woman into sex. Good women resist; bad women submit.

In both perspectives, female sexuality is repressed. Male desire, however, is a given. Females should prevent men from having sex. However, men also assume they have the right to sex. Hence, men and women can never mutually want to have sex.

In terms of economics, as capitalism emerged, women and children were excluded from the wage. This exclusion meant men still needed women to reproduce men, and women and children needed men to bring home a wage. Karl Marx and Friedrich Engels[4] saw bourgeois marriage as a form of prostitution. For Marx, an equitable sexual relationship was impossible within capitalism. Women survived in relation to men. Women took care of the household and produced the children while men worked outside the house. Only labor in the marketplace was valued economically. Wives traded sex for food and shelter.

Let me explain this concept a bit further, as it is relevant for sex, relationships, the sex trade, and reproduction. Capitalism is an economic system focused on the market. Capitalism emphasizes private ownership and the generation of profit; it requires constant economic growth. Participation in the marketplace is positive.

Several new relations emerged under capitalism. The first new relation was the wage, which replaced serf and slave ownership. Under capitalism, workers do not own the means of production, so they must work for capitalists who do. Workers sell the only thing they own, their labor power. This distinction is key because workers are not paid for the act of producing, but the ability to labor. The capitalist pays the worker for laboring for a given period of time. The payment of a wage obscures the fact that there are two aspects to this labor time. Necessary labor time is the time it takes the worker to produce enough value to buy all the commodities she/he needs for sustenance. Surplus labor time is the time the worker works beyond the necessary labor time. Surplus labor goes straight into the capitalist's pocket. A worker is not paid according to what she/he needs to survive; a worker is paid what the owner/capitalist decides is the appropriate wage for the labor time. Sometimes a wage may not even meet the "necessary," as we know with the continual need to raise the minimum wage.

The second new relation under capitalism was separating production from reproduction. "Reproduction" includes meeting the many various needs we have, from cooking and cleaning to listening to a partner vent. Under capitalism, productive labor is waged and reproductive labor is unwaged, since it appears to produce no value for the capitalist. Production was for men. Reproduction was for women.

So how might heterosexual sex be just? From an economic perspective, one could argue two things. First, women and men must have economic equality. Second, the two partners must have economic equality. However, the situation is far more complex. Economic equality is only a partial answer to the unequal power between men and women; the patriarchal assumptions would still exist. Work to end patriarchy needs to be done by all of us because the effects of patriarchy damage each of us.

Now, let's add in race and sexuality. What if you are not white and/or not heterosexual? If the emphasis is on male domination and procreation for "civilized" people, what happens if you are labeled uncivilized? Sex was inscribed into this system of male dominance and the capitalist economic system. Sex that conforms to this system is acceptable. Yet, we also have a narrative of "overpopulation" placed on Third World countries. People of other colors, people with disabilities, people who are not heterosexual are excluded from the system. Our challenge is to decide whether to include others in the current system or whether to change the system itself.

So how on earth can we have good sex? Good sex includes the positive aspects of desire, covered in the previous chapter. Good sex includes shared power without dominance or violence.

The first task in having good sex is understanding the history of negativity toward sexuality. The second task is learning to love ourselves sexually. This includes developing self-esteem. If we consider our sexual urges as negative, how can we develop self-esteem with regard to our sexuality? As Christians we need to promote love of self. This concept may sound non-Christian; however, we are told in the New Testament to "love your neighbor as yourself." You have to learn to love yourself first. Then you can learn to love the neighbor. Loving yourself fully is a good thing. Loving yourself includes respect for the self, honoring ourselves as a creation of God.

Having begun to love ourselves, we can learn to love others, to surrender to love itself. We cannot be dependent on pleasing others. With self-esteem we learn to please ourselves. Then, we move outward toward love of others. Sex can be a way to do this.

Surrender: A notion of surrender during sex seems passive at best. We tend to think of surrender as giving up. Instead, David Deida argues that surrender is "to open with no boundaries, emotional or physical, so you ease wide beyond any limiting sense of self you might have" (2002, 8). We do not surrender to another person or to pleasure but to love. This surrender is risky; all sorts of emotions may emerge: love, hate, fear, happiness, and so forth. You cannot guard your heart and love. This surrendering to love can change our daily life.

Openness: Surrendering to love requires openness. Openness during a sexual experience can be difficult. We have been taught to hide our deepest desires, to deny our desires. Yet, with practice we can open. We can let ourselves feel fully in the moment. Deida expresses this openness through the concept of communion. First, "feel your own sensations fully." Then, "feel into your lover's sensations fully." Finally, "feel through your lover into the divine" (2002, 75).

Just as we need first to build self-esteem, then learn to love others, and then simply to learn to love, the same process goes for openness in sex. We must understand the love and pleasure we have for ourself. We must understand the love and pleasure of our partner. Then we can open to the wider love and pleasure beyond the bodies. Openness can be the hardest part of a sexual experience. Usually we remain at least partly closed off.

We remain closed off, unwilling to surrender, because often we are in a setting of dominance rather than mutuality. Even when the sex between two people is mutual, there is a wider structure of inequality. If I have sex with a man, and I want him to spank me, and he does, this experience can still feel uncomfortable because of its wider social implications. I may not want anyone else to know it occurred. I may not even ask for it because of the broader implications.

What do we need to be able to achieve equality and mutuality in sex? Equality between the participants and structural equality. Structural inequality will be addressed further in the following chapter. Right now, I want to address vulnerability.

This surrender and openness leaves the participants vulnerable. Vulnerability is important in good sexual relations; however, both parties must be willing and able to be vulnerable. One cannot have power over the other. Any sexual relationship with only one vulnerable partner is unjust. Any participant in the sexual experience must fully and freely consent. Without full consent, sex is not good. Sex is coerced, forced.

To be vulnerable is to share our fears, thoughts, desires, and so forth. Women, in particular, find it difficult to make themselves deliberately vulnerable in heterosexual relationships, since women are already vulnerable in terms of patriarchy. To take one simple example, the sexual experience for heterosexual couples often ends when the male partner has ejaculated. Even here, the male determines when a sexual act ends. Women report faking orgasms to avoid disappointing the man. One does not need to orgasm to enjoy sex but one should be able to share with their partner if they would like an orgasm.

In any sexual experience, we must be safe enough to be vulnerable, to articulate what we want. This requires a framework of justice for sex: between participants and in the wider society. How can Christianity help us accomplish this?

Bible

Sex is both denigrated and celebrated in the Bible. There is certainly a lot of sex in the text! One particular text within the Jewish and Christian traditions celebrates sex: Song of Songs. Here, sex is enjoyed without inhibitions, largely from a woman's perspective.

The sex expands beyond intercourse and procreation. The lovers are not married and the female takes the lead in much of the text. For example, "I am my beloved's garden and my beloved is mine! He feeds among the lilies" (6:3). Despite the clear sexual desire and action, the Christian tradition has often distanced itself from the text's sexiness, claiming the text speaks of the relationship between God and the church. I say, even if true, the writing is using sex, a very sexy relationship, tactile, intimate, and with deep sexual longing to describe relations between God and the church. Hence, we cannot assume sex is negative here.

Several other Hebrew Bible passages celebrate sex in various ways. The Book of Ruth is one example. Widowed and in need of stability, Ruth is encouraged by her mother-in-law to seduce Boaz. She does so and marries into his family. Sex is often coded in the text. Many of us know that "to know" someone in the biblical sense is sex but we may not know that feet are often a euphemism for genitalia. Rereading the text with these and other codes in mind will surface a lot more of the sex in the text.

The New Testament, in contrast, does not celebrate sex, although the negativity toward sex can be read in different ways. For example, while Paul did prefer celibacy, he did not condemn sex altogether. Paul understood sex to be part of God's creation; however, he thought sex would disappear in heaven. Sex, however, was not completely sinful on earth.

I take several steps further and argue that although rarely discussed in such terms, the Christian narrative is pretty kinky. "If the first eve had a fetishist penchant for a serpent, the second (Mary) went for unprotected sex with a God-cloud" (Althaus-Reid[5] 2000, 23). While God impregnated Mary, any hint of sexuality and desire is missing. But what if God's impregnation of Mary caused an orgasm? Mary was, after all, connecting with the divine. Such conversations rarely occur within the Christian tradition.

Christian Tradition

In the Jewish tradition, according to the *halachah*, the traditional Jewish law, sex is allowed between a man and a woman, within marriage, through vaginal intercourse, for procreation, with regard to the religious calendar and the woman's menstrual cycle (Kahn, 264). Also, sex should be pleasurable for the woman.

This Jewish context was shared by the early Christian tradition. While the cultural norm shifted from many wives to one wife and one husband in Jewish culture, sex was still for procreation and desire was to be curbed. Further, many within the Christian tradition advocated celibacy over sex.

Early Christians had varying ideas about appropriate sexual conduct. Clement of Alexandria[6] and others argued for a middle road, both against the Gnostics who believed marriage and sex were evil and the antinomians who argued they were saved no matter their behavior. Clement argued sex was a good within marriage, for procreation. This argument held sway through Christian history.

Augustine saw sexual intercourse as negative overall. In "The Good of Marriage," he argues that while marriage is good, sex is not. For Augustine, sin brought sex into being. Perhaps without the sin, Augustine suggested, humans could have produced children without sex, just as God created the first humans or God's impregnation of Mary.

For Augustine, sex is solely for procreation. Even within marriage, he advocates the spouses stop having sex as soon as possible, by mutual consent. However, procreation mitigates the sin of sex. Sex within marriage moves sex away from desire and toward having children. "Concupiscence leads to immoderate intercourse, but in marriage it finds a means of chaste procreation. Even if it is shameful to use a husband in a lustful way, nevertheless it is honorable to choose to have sex only with a husband and to bear children only with a husband" (Augustine, 75). While sex remains sinful, procreation is honorable.

Further, each partner should be willing to have sex to help curb the other's desire and keep the other from straying outside the marriage. "Therefore, they should not deny one another that which the husband seeks from matrimony and that which the wife seeks from her husband, even if this proceeds not from a desire to have children but only from weakness and incontinence. This is to prevent them from falling into damnable seductions at the temptation of Satan because of the incontinence of one or both of them" (Augustine, 76). The sin of sex should be committed to keep one's spouse from further sin. However, one should not enjoy sex.

This aim for abstinence whenever possible became part of church tradition. Within Catholicism, married couples could have sex on less than 44 days a year if they followed the restrictions on sex during particular religious days and followed the woman's menstrual cycle (Roeber, 8). In another example, Saint Ambrose (337–397 CE), bishop of Milan, extended the enforcement of sex for procreation to banning sex while the woman was pregnant.

In case I've been unclear, the church tradition did not celebrate sex. It tolerated sex for procreation. Within this attempt at procreation, the woman was to be passive, focused on getting pregnant. Any desire within this act was sinful; the sex act itself was impure but it could be forgiven under these conditions.

The confession manuals used throughout the centuries confirm this negative obsession. The Penitentials, for example, used from the sixth through the twelfth centuries, provided a list of sins and penances that priests used for confession. Every sexual act apart from sexual intercourse within marriage for procreation was sinful and needed to be confessed. Foucault notes that as confession became less important in people's lives, medicine and psychiatry became more important, continuing the obsession with sex and its presumed negativity.

Today, we still see evidence of these. To take just one example, let's consider abstinence campaigns. Before marriage, sex is sinful. If you have sex before marriage, you ruin yourself for the future marriage. Nowhere do these campaigns teach about healthy sexual relationships, but simply that sex should occur after marriage. Here too, there is an obsession with sex, prohibited before marriage, purported to be amazing after marriage without any effort.

Theology

In light of this history, we have some work to do regarding sex. First, let us reiterate that sexual desire is positive. Desire is God-given and should be cultivated. Neither desire nor sex is inherently sinful. Sin enters the equation when we treat another unjustly. Good sex treats others justly.

In sex, we enter into a relation with another person. Our body is in relation with another body. Hopefully, our mind/emotions/soul is as well. What should this relation include?

Play: Playfulness is one component to sex often missing from our conversations, whether secular or religious. Sex seems to be serious business. However, sex should involve joy and pleasure because we are celebrating life and knowing each other. Since joy within sex seems obvious, why is it missing from our discussion? Why does the Christian tradition neglect and disparage sex?

Humans were created for play and enjoyment. Work only came into the equation after the fall in the Garden of Eden, according to the Hebrew Bible. God desires us and created us to desire each other. Play is part of this desire to know each other, nature, and God. Play was part of the Sabbath, sexual play too for married couples.[7] So the play of sex can be part of the tradition.

This notion can bring us back to sex as a way to know and delight in the other. As we grow from children to adults, we tend to dismiss play but play is central to knowing and enjoying each other. As children we most usually play with others. We learn to share and care about others. This knowledge can be translated to our sexual experiences. We can learn to care about each other through play in sex. This play heightens attention to ourselves and to the other, crucial to develop into full human beings in community.

Shifting the understanding of sex as a way to know the other through playing means the "goal" is not orgasm. Sex is also about enjoying the other and their pleasure. The clitoris is one example of this. Its purpose is enjoyment, nothing else. A woman does not need a clitoris biologically. Yet, she was created with one. Thinking of sex as playful knowing opens up the spectrum of what sex can be. Sex is all the attention we give to a sexual partner, to their pleasure and to our own. This is the same for desire. The goal is to enjoy desire; desire will continue through the pleasure of knowing.

In this way, we communicate with each other and with God. In playing with each other, we come to know each other. This communion and union brings us closer to God. Sex is not limited to one event or one person. Sex is an important piece of knowing. Pleasure and play within sex is critical for knowing. Yet, we will never fulfill our desire; we only achieve it in small moments. We begin to know but we will never know fully. The point is the process of knowing and attending to each other. Sex is part of communion, communion with God, which we celebrate through the Eucharist as well.

Communion: Thinking of sex as play and the Eucharist can seem paradoxical but in play with each other we come to know God. Communion is a moment of celebrating this union, through the body and blood of Christ. We make room in ourselves for God; we ingest part of the divine. We open ourselves to God.[8] Sex and the Eucharist are ways of communing with God.

We can also see this communion when Thomas touches the risen Christ. Thomas doubts Jesus is really present and Jesus invites Thomas to touch him. Thomas touches Jesus. Each of us is invited to touch God through touching others. Touching is a means of communion, sexual as well as spiritual. Communion with God occurs through the spectrum of our lives, not just in the Eucharist. We taste and we touch. As with the Song of Songs, tasting is one of the delights of life; we taste God in the Eucharist; we taste our lovers in sex.

Touching occurs in many parts of our lives; it has a sexual component. Sexuality is positive. Touching increases our communion. We tend to maintain a sharp divide between sexual touching and platonic touching but it is along a spectrum. The brush of a hand on a shoulder can be uncomfortable, when unwanted. The same brush of a hand can be incredibly wanted. This touching is intensified in sexual intercourse. However well or poorly one knows a partner, sex communicates nearness. Nearness can be dangerous as well as pleasurable. Hence, we need to draw near to each other with care and mutuality. Consent is crucial for communion, to knowing God. Touch is not the problem itself; it is the relationship between those touching.

This consent combined with shared power is critical to be able to be vulnerable. In sex, one person enters another; one person makes room for another within themselves, in mouths and other places. While we celebrate nearness to another in sex; we also become vulnerable.

Sacred: Sex is holy. Sex is a place where we can find God. I didn't begin with this concept; I began with play because our notion of the holy can be serious and somewhat intimidating. I want us to move from play to holiness to remember the sacred can also be enjoyable and the enjoyable can be sacred. Sex is holy because we come know God in all our messy physical and spiritual components. Sex reminds us our bodies are holy. We experience God through sex. Sex is commonly seen as an escape from life. However, in contrast, sex is in the fullness of life. It is a way to deeply know others and God. When we participate in sex, as in communion, we are knowing God.

We celebrate ourselves, the other, and God. In one set of marriage vows, each person states: "with my body I thee worship." In sex and in life we share ourselves, our bodies, and our minds with others. As the body and blood of Christ are sacred, so too are our bodies to each other. In sex, however ordinary, we find the extraordinariness of each other and of God.

Sex becomes a form of worship in this attention to ourselves, to another, and to God. We find ourselves in the other and in God and vice versa. How different would our sex lives be if we thought of them as playful worship?

Sex is simply one way of enjoying God and others. Sex does not fulfill desire, but it expresses desire. Sex does not provide happiness, but it expresses happiness. Sex does not provide love, but it expresses love. Sex is simply part of the process of knowing others and God. We do not have to work to find God in sex; God is simply present. In paying attention to the other through sex, we are also in God's presence. We begin to understand communion and community. Sex gives us one opportunity to learn how to be in community. Sex is one place where we can experience intimacy, joy, desire, and pleasure on a small scale and learn to pay that kind of attention to the larger community of God's creatures. We often think of sex with another person as the most intimate we should be but these practices of joy and desire should be ways of communicating in the larger community. We can relate to more than one individual. The following chapter will focus on partnership and relations in community that could emerge from this celebration of sex.

Act

1. Have good sex. Have mutually pleasurable, mutually empowering sex.
2. Have good sexual relationships. Good sexual relationships begin with protecting ourselves as we get to know another. We slowly open to another. This process of exploring ourselves and others need not have marriage as its goal. Instead, the goal is to know God through knowing others. We will consider this further in the next chapter but for now, think about having sex with someone who peaks your interest, who you can talk to, with whom you would like to explore pleasure.
3. Understand there is a spectrum of sexual relationships. Rather than list who you can and cannot have sex with, I suggest any relationship should be mutual.
4. Use sex and sexuality as a source for justice. We need to learn to connect with others in all ways. Consider volunteering, joining a grassroots network. The more we learn what we are passionate about, how we connect with others, the better we know ourselves and our desires, sexual and all. When we understand and practice good sex, this way of knowing another can lead us to use our deepest desires to work toward

justice. Sex can teach us to love mutually, for the good of each other. We can learn to have mature relationships in all areas of our life. Mature relationships go beyond the axiom "first do no harm." Relationships improve our self-understanding, self-respect, and the understanding of and respect for others. They teach us how to share power and pleasure. All of this can help us to work toward justice: for ourselves and for others. Every human being in the world deserves to love and to be loved. Sex is an expression of love and good sex is an example of how to live justly in the world.

5. Work to end racism, sexism, classism, heterosexism, and ableism. The more just our structures are, the more just our relationships will be, the easier it will be to have good sex. Because good sex requires equality and mutuality between the participants, our wider structures need to be just so that we can enter into just relationships.
6. Finally, know that you do not have to have sex. We need to work toward a world where sex is always consensual. Each of us needs to be able to decide who we touch and who touches us. When justice is enacted, this decision will be much easier.

Sex is a way to know God but we need to release sex from its current unjust situation.

Moving Forward

Sex is not about what body part goes where at any particular moment. Good sex is about the larger context around the acts. This context includes the entire community. I'll engage this piece as we move into the next chapter. For now, let's address the people having sex.

1. Each person must freely consent. In order to begin to know others and to know God, anyone involved in sexual contact, whether spiritual, physical, or emotional, must consent. Each person must consent at any point in the process and at any point in the relationship. Consent is more than saying yes. Consent from partners means each will fully participate and enable any other to fully participate. For example: "Would you like to fool around with me?" "Yes, I would." "I'm not really sure what I want yet but I'd like to explore you a bit." "Sounds good. Let's check in as we go and see what we want."

"Ok." … and continue communicating through the process. If it feels awkward to talk, it will probably feel awkward to have sex. These are signs that one should pause and think.

2. There must be mutuality. Mutuality does not mean doing the same thing for each other, evoking the same feelings in each other. Mutuality means that any parties involved agree they are receiving what they want and giving what they want. Consent and mutuality are the basis for true intimacy. As your own needs and desires are respected and attended to, you open further, enabling you to respond to another's needs and desires. We tend to close ourselves off in sex. Either we don't want to feel too much or we don't want others outside (and sometimes within) the sexual act to know what we have felt. To share joy and pleasure with others, we need to feel safe and respected. This mutuality enables communion. We want each person to know God. To know God we must know others. Sex is as much about the other(s) as about the self.
3. Power must be shared between the participants. The next chapter addresses this further. We need to overturn our patriarchal society, for example. The male does not have to be active and the female passive. Not only does this privilege heterosexuality, but even within heterosexual relationships, the partners should be equal participants.
4. There must be a level of trust, discussed honestly. Each person must be able to express what they want and each must be able to trust the other. This can be called a covenant. However, trust must be developed. No one can automatically trust another, even with consent. Trust builds over a sexual experience or a sexual relationship. One learns to trust as the other responds. One can have good sex without complete trust but one will have better sex as trust deepens. One starts to build trust only after beginning to know another. Caution is a good thing but one does not have to wait for all sexual experiences. Full consent is a good beginning to building trust. Barbara Blodgett[9] introduces the concept of "friendly distrust." Friendly distrust is about learning to trust but protecting yourself and your partner at the same time. Trust is built as a relationship lengthens but relationships also build trust, so a level of distrust is also crucial when entering a relationship.

5. Good sex involves play, joy, and pleasure, as I argued earlier. These practices are how we come to know God, how we engage the holy and the sacred.
6. The sexual relationship should be just within itself and within the wider community. Sex happens not just between two individuals but within the community as a whole. We tend to separate our sex lives from our community lives but all of our experiences are along the spectrum of knowing each other. Love is what bonds a community together. Sexual desire is a part of love. As a society as a whole, we tend to proscribe certain sexual behaviors and relationships to try to contain excess desire. At the same time, we want people to live in community and love each other. Teaching us all how to love and how to desire, rather than proscribing behavior, is critical here. The next chapter will consider partnership more broadly to think about what sex should look like within the broader community.

   Sex is a part of the entire community. This perspective may come up against the notion that sex should be about individual choice but all our choices are in community and they affect the community for better or for worse. To consider justice and inequality in the broader community is also crucial. It is difficult to have a relationship between equals where power is shared in light of the economic, racial, gender-based, religious, and other types of discrimination that exist.

   Good sex empowers ourselves and others.

Questions for Reflection

1. How would you define "having good sex?"
2. I argued that sex should involve play, communion, and the sacred. Which aspect resonated most with you and why?
3. In "Moving Forward," I suggested there are six aspects to "good" sex? Which did not appear in your own definition and why do you think you excluded them?

Further Suggested Readings

Deida, David. 2002. *Finding God Through Sex*. Boulder: Sounds True.

Deida's excellent book explores the connection between spirituality and sex through attention to particular sexual practices. He articulates the importance of surrender, openness, and desire for both partners and shows how this is attainable in our sex lives.

Deida, David. 2007. *The Enlightened Sex Manual: Sexual Skills for the Superior Lover.* Boulder: Sounds True.

This book takes an even more practical approach toward good sex by exploring practices that increase the attention to spiritual energy during sex. It is divided into three sections: Energy, Orgasm, and Variations in sexual practices.

Ellison, Marvin. "What Makes 'Good Sex' Good?" In Ellison, Marvin 2012. *Making Love Just: Sexual Ethics for Perplexing Times.* Minneapolis: Fortress Press, 23–39.

In this concise yet detailed chapter, Ellison explores the history of Christian negativity toward sex as well as modern-day critiques of sex in the Christian churches. His chapter offers an alternative sexual ethic as the basis for deciding when to have sex and with whom.

Notes

1. Deida is a writer on sex and spirituality.
2. Foucault was a French philosopher who lived from 1926 to 1984.
3. Galen was a Greek physician and philosopher who lived from about 130 to 210 CE.
4. Marx was a Prussian philosopher, economist, and political theorist who lived from 1818 to 1883. Engels, with whom Marx collaborated, was also a German philosopher (1820–1895).
5. Marcella Althaus-Reid was an Argentinian feminist liberation theologian and Chair of Contextual Theology at the University of Edinburgh, UK, until her death in 2009.
6. Clement lived from *c.* 110 to 215 CE, a convert to Christianity and theologian.
7. "Many historical Jewish traditions encourage married couples to play with one another in sex on the Sabbath, in the lingering rest that that day promises" (Jensen, 69).
8. "Our most tangible act in the Eucharist is when we take Christ's body into our own, making room for the One who desires us as he penetrates us. … In the Eucharist, we open ourselves to Christ (taking him in our mouths) as Christ opens to us, and we are opened by him" (Jensen, 85).
9. Blodgett is an ethicist, minister in the United Church of Christ, and professor at Lexington Theological Seminary.

References

Abbott, Elizabeth. 2010. *A History of Marriage: From Same Sex Unions to Private Vows and Common Law, the Surprising Diversity of a Tradition*. New York: Seven Stories Press.

Althaus-Reid, Marcella. 2000. *Indecent Theology: Theological Perversions in Sex, Gender and Politics*. London: Routledge.

Augustine, St. 2002. From the Good of Marriage. In *Theology and Sexuality: Classic and Contemporary Readings*, ed. E. Rogers Jr., 71–86. Malden: Blackwell.

Deida, David. 2002. *Finding God Through Sex*. Boulder: Sounds True.

———. 2007. *The Enlightened Sex Manual: Sexual Skills for the Superior Lover*. Boulder: Sounds True.

Ellison, Marvin. 2012. What Makes "Good Sex" Good? In *Making Love Just: Sexual Ethics for Perplexing Times*, ed. Marvin Ellison, 23–39. Minneapolis: Fortress Press.

Foucault, Michel. 1990. *The History of Sexuality: Volume 1: An Introduction*. Trans. Robert Hurley. New York: Vintage Books.

Jensen, David. 2013. *God, Desire, and a Theology of Human Sexuality*. Louisville: Westminster John Knox Press.

Kahn, Yoel. 2010. Making Love as Making Justice: Towards a New Jewish Ethic of Sexuality. In *Sexuality and the Sacred*, ed. Marvin M. Ellison and Kelly Brown Douglas, 2nd ed., 262–271. Louisville: Westminster John Knox Press.

Roeber, A.G. 2012. *Hopes for Better Spouses: Protestant Marriage and Church Renewal in Early Modern Europe, India, and North America*. Grand Rapids: Eerdmans.

Rubio, Julie Hanlon. 2010. The Practice of Sex in Christian Marriage. In *Leaving and Coming Home: New Wineskins for Catholic Sexual Ethics*, ed. David Cloutier, 226–249. Eugene: Cascade Books.

CHAPTER 4

Partnership

Abstract While the Christian tradition has suggested marriage is the appropriate locus for sexual relationships, many people are not married and many married couples are not in good relationships. This chapter begins from our understandings of sexual desire and good sex to articulate what good sexual relationships could look like. Rejecting the focus on marriage, the chapter argues for reframing relationships around a deeper notion of friendship. It begins with a definition of marriage, explores the historical context around marriage, and articulates how to have a good partnership with reference to the biblical tradition, the Christian tradition, and theology.

Keywords Partnership • Marriage • Friendship • Adultery • Covenant

Who should we have sex with and when? The Christian tradition has assumed the context should be marriage. We need to subject marriage to suspicion. Our church traditions mistakenly supported slavery, considered homosexuality to be sinful, and so forth. What other mistaken assumptions might the Christian tradition hold? What are the theological principles we can use today to figure out what our partnerships could look like? Could we base our sexual ethics on friendship rather than marriage? This chapter will examine what our friendships and partnerships might look like if we celebrated desire and sex as a way to know God.

T. Cooper, *A Christian Guide to Liberating Desire, Sex, Partnership, Work, and Reproduction*,
https://doi.org/10.1007/978-3-319-70896-6_4

In recent years, the focus on marriage was on accepting same-sex partners. This goal was achieved. Yet, I think it is tinged with sadness. Why reify marriage? Why not reject marriage as a patriarchal and property-related harmful tradition? In adapting marriage to include same-sex couples, we further support the hegemonic notion of marriage, instead of extending the benefits of partnership to others outside the marriage contract. Rather than trying to adjust marriage to include more people, should we abandon marriage as the measuring stick for relationships? Including same-sex couples in marriage does not upend marriage itself.

Marriage is an unjust privilege. Marriage is a means of social control, legitimating or delegitimating relationships. I do not assume that heterosexual marriage is the appropriate framework for sexual relationships. Rather, I ask, what can sexual relationships look like from a Christian perspective? Each relationship must be based on consent, mutuality, joy, and the other pieces I noted in the previous chapter. So working from our experience and our understanding of sex and desire as positive ways to know God, let's rethink friendship, partnership, and marriage.

Definition

I begin with two definitions of marriage, both unsatisfactory.

1. The Massachusetts Supreme Judicial Court, in November 2003, defined marriage as "the voluntary union of two persons as spouses, to the exclusion of all others" (Qtd. in Ellison 2012, 64).
2. Marvin Ellison[1] himself defines marriage as "the covenanted or vowed union of two persons as committed life partners" (Ellison 2012, 63).

I question whether the concept of "two," "exclusion," and "life partners" needs to be part of sexual relationships. Instead, I'll work to describe what sexual partnerships could consist of throughout the chapter.

Historical Context

Marriage was important within the Jewish tradition. Where Judaism focused on one God, the surrounding cultures had male and female gods, celebrating fertility through sex. Humans who procreated were imitating the divinities, participating in a divine action. People celebrated the fertility of humans, gods, animals, and plants, along with sex. In contrast, the God of the Jewish and later Christian tradition was not in partnership with another god, removing sex from the divine equation.

For the early Jewish population, marriage was to produce children, to know paternity. A child's paternity was critical to carry on the family name and pass on inheritance. If a man wanted another woman, he could add her as a wife. Women, however, could only have sex with the one husband. If a man had sex with another man's wife, the man was stealing the husband's property. Marriage was for procreation; children carried on the father's line; children within marriage made sure the lineage was secure.

Living as a minority in others' land for much of their history, it was important for the Jewish people to expand and control their population through family lineage. For example, if a woman's husband died, a brother-in-law would take her as his wife. Divorce was rare as men could have multiple wives.

Adultery was having sex with a married woman. Having sex with an unmarried woman violated the property rights of her father. Having sex with a married woman violated the property rights of her husband.[2] Men, however, could take on additional wives, if they could provide for the expanding family. Men could have sex with their own property, whether wives or slaves. The woman could only have sex with her husband.

The practice of polygamy disappeared as the Greek culture of one man and one woman in marriage took over. During the time of the New Testament, divorce became an issue because men could not add another wife. A woman's situation became more precarious, as she could be discarded. In this context, the New Testament critiques divorce.

In the surrounding Greek and Roman culture, wives, concubines, and mistresses were all common. A husband was required to have sex with his wife to procreate. However, he could have sex outside the marriage boundaries, though not with a married woman, as she was another's property. The law also distinguished between raping a married woman and seducing her. Seduction was worse because, more than an overwhelming bodily desire, it was a deliberate attempt to take another's property. While a man could no longer have multiple wives, he could still have multiple sexual partners. The woman still could only have sex with her husband. The wife's role was to submit; the husband's role was to dominate.

Within the Christian tradition, the emphasis shifted from marriage for procreation to remaining celibate, although the culture in New Testament times still viewed marriage as an important part of continuing the family line.

Marriage did not unite a man and woman in love. Instead, marriage was a family affair, arranged by relatives, to support the community.

Over time, marriage became a more complicated status to attain within Christian "lands." In the first millennium, a man and a woman could simply say they were married. Beginning in 1025, people were required to marry formally within the church, rather than let the church know they were married, though this news took a while to trickle down to the bulk of the population (Roeber, 10). The church also charged for the marriage ceremony, excluding people who could not afford the fees.

When Christianity entered Latin America through colonization, it enforced its particular notions of marriage and sex. Colonial men married women of European descent and used native women as mistresses. These relationships were known as "*mala vida* (bad living)," because of their violence (Althaus-Reid 2000, 20–21). Women were under the dominion of their spouses sexually and economically.

As regions of Europe became Protestant, the state officially recognized marriage while the church blessed the joining of the couple. Church and state were separated but both were required to approve the marriage. Marriage became even more difficult to attain; one had to pay the church and the state to be married. In practice, marriage remained a means for procreation and the continuation of families. Many couples never married formally in Europe and North America. In the USA, wealthy white European-descended Protestants married but, often, Africans, Asians, Native Americans, and the poor were excluded. Official marriage was a status reserved for those wealthy enough to pass on the family name and property, although within the church it was the only union allowed between a man and a woman. So many people were excluded, forced into "sin."[3] In North America, as in Europe, marriage remained a privilege.

In addition, many couples formally married when the woman became pregnant. While elite men and women did often marry before they had sex, the common people did not. When people got engaged, they started to have sex and the marriage process was cemented by pregnancy. What we see as normal within the Christian tradition today was limited to the elite minority.

Further, the rules regulating sex before marriage became stricter over time. Under the Hardwick Marriage Act of 1753, all marriages had to be registered in England. Elite women were supposed to be virgins at the time of the ceremony (Thatcher, 241). Virginity became a measure of status. When elite women reached marital age, they had a "coming out" party and marriage with women wearing white became the norm for the elite. The white dress symbolized purity. This purity became the marker of status. The concept of a honeymoon began, as the couple got to know each other intimately after the wedding ceremony.

In the colonial USA, marriage was still a mostly informal process. A couple was considered married once the woman became pregnant. Racism also became the rule of the day. Whites could not marry people of color, whether African or Caribbean slaves, indigenous Americans, or Asians. Forty-one states had laws against interracial marriage, until the Supreme Court finally overturned them in the 1960s.

Yet, mixed-race children were common, particularly in the South. A South Carolina planter's wife named Mary Boykin Chesnut wrote: "Like the patriarchs of old, our men live all in one house with their wives and concubines; and the mulattoes one sees in every family partly resembled the white children" (qtd. in Abbott, 132–33). The white male slave owners had sex with the slave women, had children with them, and kept them in the household. The wives lived under these conditions, while the slave women were forced to procreate with the owner.

Further, those enslaved could not marry. Subject to the whims of their masters, and not considered fully human, the slaves held no rights under the law. This situation was the start of the long history of the female-headed black household, still in place today with the high rates of incarceration of African-American men in the USA. The masters decided when to sell and keep slaves without consideration for any partnership a slave might have. The slave owners also decided which slaves needed to procreate with each other to breed more slaves.

By the end of the nineteenth century, marriage had changed for the white community both in the USA and in Europe, due to the exponential increase in life expectancy. While in 1711 in England, men died on average at 32, by 1831, it was 44, and by the end of the century, it was in their late 50s. In the twentieth century, the upward trend has continued, with men living on average until 74 and women until 80 years (Abbott, 106). This longer lifespan changes the character of a "life-long" marriage. A lifetime of marriage was no longer 5–10 years but could be more than 50.

For much of history many people have been unable to be officially "married." So, when the Christian tradition argues that marriage is the space for sex and procreation, it excludes many people. Many people have nurturing and healthy relationships outside of marriage. Many families survive and thrive without marriage.

In the USA and Europe today, many people remain unmarried. In the USA, as of 2005, 50% of women and 47% of men were not in married households. Married couples are often a minority, despite marriage being considered a cornerstone of society.

Hermeneutical Circle

See: Marriage and Friendship Today

First, let us note that criticizing marriage goes against the grain for many people today. In Western society, the idea of a nuclear family with a husband, wife, and children is predominant. If much is at stake with redefining marriage, even more is at stake if we suggest getting rid of it. Marriage is seen as the framework for Western society, influencing economics, politics, and so forth. Though it "orders" our society, many people order their lives without marriage.

Marriage takes on a mythical status, defined "ideally" rather than on the reality of people's situations. Anyone unmarried is less in status. Not everyone can marry. Marriage's borders are well protected. But if many people are not married, marriage becomes a mythical cornerstone. Further, many married people are not in life-giving relationships. Marriage itself is no insurance against harm.

Second, the assumption that sex is only allowed within marriage for procreation means people are suddenly able to have sex after having been denied for their entire lives. In a moment, one moves from a situation of "thou shalt not" to "go have sex and make babies with wild abandon." As many couples who waited until the wedding night know, that is pressure! There is no education on how to switch from denying all desire to sharing desire with one's spouse, as I noted in the previous chapter.

Third, there is a myth that one only becomes complete when joined to another in marriage. Any individual outside of marriage is seen as less than whole. Within marriage, this concept is dangerous too. If the spouse is to complete the other, and the male is dominant over the female, then in a heterosexual marriage, the female completes the male. Yet, when two people enter a relationship it should be mutually empowering. These two people remain two, with their differing desires, needs, and so forth. Often, marriage is seen as the "end" of the development process. However, both individuals continue to grow, need to be nurtured, and to nurture. All of this takes work. Instead, people often view marriage as finding the "one" who will complete them. After marriage, one is supposed to be complete; this view is stagnant and incorrect.

Women in particular lose their identities in marriage. Women report feeling more in control in nonmarital relationships rather than in marriages. While women feel they have the ability to start or end a relationship and be as attached as they want to a partner, control is lost within a heterosexual marriage.

Fourth, while many people state they are against adultery, they still have sex outside the bounds of their own marriage. The majority of partners in a marriage report having extramarital sex: 55% of women and 65% of men (Ellison 2012, 49).

Fifth, committing to marriage for a lifetime today is much longer than in any other time throughout history. As life expectancies have risen, lifelong marriages are no longer 10 or so years on average but 50 or more. The two partners are expected to change in accordance with each other for this lengthy lifetime.

Sixth, modern marriage is assumed to be based on love. Throughout history, it was assumed love would grow between people chosen as spouses by their families. One did not choose to marry out of love, rather one would come to love the one she/he married over time. Of course, this notion also resided within the gender hierarchy of a man over a woman.

Seventh, the marital relationship is assumed to be the only relationship needed. Throughout history, marriage was considered in community to be a match between families. While this concept may be problematic in many ways, the removal of marriage from community is also problematic. With the notion of completion in marriage comes an assumption that nothing is needed outside the partnership. All pressure moves to the spouse to meet needs and desires. Yet, friendships and families need to be cultivated to help our communities grow. Marriage should open us further to community life. In a partnership, we learn on a small scale how to interact with the community on a larger scale. The pressure put on marriage today to answer all problems is doomed to failure. Throughout history, marriage was seen as part of a network on relationships in community. No one relationship can take the place of the broader community; all our relationships are in community.

Considering Friendship

If we think of sexual acts as a spectrum from touching to intercourse, then we can consider too that our friendships contain some aspect of sexual knowing and desire. This seems suspect when the only proper relationship is considered to be between two people within marriage. However, once we open the horizon to knowing others as a way to know God, we can then discuss friendship within this context.

Friendship whether platonic or with benefits is a relationship between sexual people. Failing to discuss sex and desire can be detrimental to every relationship. On the one hand, we assume friendship is asexual. On the other hand, friendships become suspect within marriage, particularly friendships between a man and a woman, if both are heterosexual. Part of this trouble with understanding friendship stems from the assumption that any sexual connection will lead to sex, which will destroy other relationships. Rather than seeing humans as sexual beings, with a spectrum of sexual expression, the aim is to repress sexuality except within marriage.

What is true of sexual relationships is true of friendships as well. Friendship should be consensual and mutual. So too should relations within the wider community. We need to learn to be intimate in our relationships, whether they include sex or not. Intimacy includes a safe space where one can be vulnerable and open. Friendships need work to continue to grow; they require time, effort, and play. Whether one sees a friend every day or once a year, the relationship can grow or remain stable. Shared experiences, openness, and space to be vulnerable are all part of this relationship. Friendship also cultivates desire.

Judge

Academics

Marriage in the West was until recently limited to one man and one woman. In the past few years, same-sex marriage has come into law. Racism still persists and often mixed-race marriages are looked down upon; the same is true for mixed religions within marriage. Here, we begin with gender inequality within marriage and the question of limitation to two partners.

Gender Issues

Within a marriage between a man and a woman, the woman is vulnerable due to the privilege a male assumes within patriarchy. She is vulnerable because she lacks power and an individual identity. Sometimes this vulnerability leads to violence against women.

First, let's consider the economic piece. In our capitalist system, marriage has enabled men to work outside the home while women manage the home and raise the children. Thus, women's economic status depends on the man's ability to earn a wage. Women's work in the home is unpaid and considered irrelevant to the market. However, women's work impacts the ability of the male to participate in the workplace. While far more women enter the workplace now than 40 years ago, the inequalities of home life continue. Most women are still expected to do the lion's share of the domestic work, unremunerated work. Well-off families can hire domestic workers to clean and take care of the children. These workers are mainly women taking time away from their own families. The final chapter considers this inequality further.

Second, women's sexuality is expected to disappear after marriage and children. While women are supposed to make themselves attractive in order to get a husband, after women marry they are supposed to become mothers. A mother and wife is asexualized. Men, then, no longer desire their wives but other women. Within many cultures, a man can have mistresses. The wives, however, must have no sexual urges or certainly not give in to them. Magically the man and woman know how to have great sex upon getting married but then, after having children, the wife is to have no more sexual urges. Men, however, can.

Third, women also take on the majority of the emotional and organizational work of the relationship. Studies show that men tend to have fewer deep friendships than women do. In fact, men have fewer friendships overall. Within marriage, this discrepancy intensifies. Two things occur. First, the pressure is put on the marital partners to meet all of each other's needs. Second, women lose more friendships than men do, simply by having more before. Male independence is encouraged, while in reality the women shoulder the burden of the emotional weight of both people. Women often are responsible for the home, in all its emotional, reproductive, and organizational realms. Yet, this labor remains unseen. Men in heterosexual relationships assume they are independent but they actually leave the management of the emotions and other burdens of the relationship to the women. Women become responsible for the man's happiness, leaving little time to cultivate their own.

Finally, we move to an area rarely discussed: abuse within marriage. We know rape within marriage can occur; however, there is far more to a healthy relationship than the absence of rape. There is also the problem of domestic abuse: physical, verbal, and emotional. In the USA, statistics show one in four women suffers from domestic abuse; one in six women has been raped. Further, rape occurs in 45% of relationships of domestic abuse.[4] Marriage is not a haven from the world; much of the violence against women takes place within a marriage. Almost 40% of reported rapes occur within marriage.[5] Given these statistics, we cannot assume marriage is the best relationship possible.

We need to address the burdens of women within heterosexual marriage.

Current Cultural Issues: The Two-Person Assumption

Should a sexual relationship be limited to two people? I have already stated we need to consider sexuality within friendships. Let's take this one step further and ask whether one could be in sexual relationship with more than one person. Traditionally, we assume a long-term sexual relationship, particularly marriage, should be sexually exclusive. Yet, does faithfulness to a partner have to include never having sex with another person? I would say no and so would some other sexual ethicists. One could fully commit to a partner and still have sex outside that relationship. If we acknowledge that the chosen partner cannot meet all our needs, for example, for friendship, why must the partner meet all our sexual needs?

There are four underlying assumptions for limiting sex to two partners: (1) we cannot love more than one person; (2) sex with anyone else will destroy that love; (3) the relationship with one person should provide all we need; and (4) only weak/bad people will have sex outside of this relationship.[6]

Having sex with someone other than your partner is seen as betrayal. If so many people have sex outside of their own marriages and stay in their marriages, could it be possible for this not to be betrayal? What if you did want to be in a relationship for 50–60 years? What might you need outside this relationship? One needs multiple relationships to come to know God; any relationship may or may not become sexual. With honesty in the process, the primary relationship could grow and thrive.

Adultery is having a sexual relationship outside of marriage. It is not the same as being unfaithful. Being unfaithful is anything that breaches the honesty and agreement between the partners. It is breaking whatever commitment was agreed upon by the partners. Being faithful could include outside relationships. In any relationship, one should be committed to that friendship or partnership. This commitment may or may not exclude sexual intimacy with another person. The relationship should be mutual and maintain honesty and consent at all times.

Limiting sex to one relationship is arbitrary and a means of control. Marriage, in particular, is a means of social control. Adultery then becomes an escape from a relationship, set up to fail. Rather than assuming marriage as the ideal relationship to order society, let's rethink what our relationships should look like ethically and let that produce a just society.

Women lose much in a heterosexual marriage that excludes other relationships. The secrecy and lack of ability to make decisions damage a relationship, not any particular act or lack thereof. Multiple relationships may be one way for a woman to ensure mutuality, or at least to ensure not being "owned" by another person.

Finally, commitment to another person need not be for a lifetime. People change over time. There is nothing wrong with moving in and out of relationships. Friendships and relationships ebb and flow, as do communities. We cannot assume permanence as a precondition for sexual relationships.

What might it look like to have multiple relationships, friendships, and partnerships? There are a variety of relationships apart from a sexual partnership with one person for life. For example, one could have a friendship with sex. *Amigovio* is a concept emerging in Argentina (Althaus-Reid 2000, 142–44). This word is comprised of the word for friend and for boyfriend/girlfriend. *Amigovio* is a form of sexual relationship and friendship. People remain in relationship whether the sex continues or not. This relationship carries no stigma. One may have a sexual relationship for a time and then not. The sexual nature of the relationship is fluid rather than set.

Further, a heterosexual woman could partner with more than one man. One feminist Muslim theologian suggests polygyny. Polygyny counters the problem of few male partners due to incarceration rates of black men (Ellison 2012, 51). US society has made it difficult for African-American women to marry African-American men and actually live with them by incarcerating so many black men for so long. Thus, women must either marry outside their race, remain outside the bonds of marriage, marry someone who may never leave prison, or think outside the box. In difficult economic, political, racial, and gendered situations, multiple relationships could be a good option. Since polygamy was never officially condemned in the biblical tradition, what about one wife and multiple husbands?

Another option is an "open marriage," where one commits to a person but can also have other friendships and relationships, known as monogamy-plus. The marital relationship remains primary and other relationships are permitted as long as the partners are open and honest. Dishonesty breaks a commitment, not sexual acts themselves. One can commit to a primary relationship, with the possibility of others developing.

One other suggestion for marriage comes from a Tanzanian woman named Grace. In a conversation where women were imagining what marriage would be like if they could decide, she suggested marriage as a contract, lasting three to five years. The contract could be renewable, enabling women to ensure the marriage was positive for them (Browning, 153).

Finally, one can be in multiple relationships at the same time, without any one relationship having to take priority over others: polyamory. Polyamory is based on friendships with many people, which can become sexual or not depending on the situation and time. This style of relationship acknowledges one can love more than one person. The commitment is to each person involved in the relationship and this commitment requires honesty and mutual consent. The key to any relationship is honesty and mutuality. Let's explore how the Bible, tradition, and theology could help us.

Bible

I discussed this theme in the introduction, so I will only place a few reminders here. In the Hebrew Bible, the goal was procreation to continue the male line; multiple wives and sex with slaves were permitted. In the New Testament, the argument for marriage is limited to controlling sexual desire, though celibacy was preferred. The goal of procreation disappeared with the assumption of Christ's imminent return.

There are certain contradictions in the way we assume marriage is based on biblical tradition. For example, Adam and Eve are often celebrated as the first marriage. Yes, one version of the text states they were the first humans created. Yet, it is a partnership, not an official marriage, and there was little choice involved.

Further, the Gospels offer different perspectives on marriage. Luke presents Jesus as against marriage, while Matthew 19:4–6 and Mark 10:6–9 state that marriage is ordained by God. Paul prefers people to remain unmarried but permits it if people cannot otherwise control their desire for sex (1 Cor. 7:8). Here, marriage can be a good when used to control desire. In the context of the New Testament, Jesus was expected to return. Thus, the only reason to marry would be if one could not control one's own sexual urges; there was no need for procreation. Marriage is a stopgap; it will not exist in the new heaven and new earth.

In the New Testament view, the man is still prioritized over the woman, particularly in the Pauline letters. Wives are expected to obey their husbands. See, for example, Eph. 5:22. One text providing a more equal view, however, is I Corinthians 7:3–4, though the text contains a disturbing notion of ownership. At least this ownership is of both over each other: "The husband should give to his wife her conjugal rights, and likewise the wife to her husband. For the wife does not have authority and control over her own body, but the husband; likewise also the husband does not have authority and control over his body, but the wife." Here, they are responsible for each other.

Christian Tradition

The early church fathers preferred celibacy over marriage. However, marriage was still allowed for procreation and as a place to control desire. The early church tradition also excluded polygamy, though it is never condemned in the biblical text. Church theologians acknowledged they were not following the biblical text in this prohibition. Augustine argued that in the Old Testament, men married more than one woman because the community needed to reproduce, which was unnecessary now. So, he acknowledged a difference in time could mean a different interpretation. Martin Luther[7] also acknowledged that polygamy was not prohibited in the biblical text; however, he suggested Christians should sometimes avoid things permitted in the biblical text. So theologians kept the Hebrew Bible's focus on procreation, ignored its use of polygamy, and ignored the societal norm of several mistresses. This restriction on marriage had negative effects on women in particular. Women could be "owned" by men as mistresses, without the protection or status of a wife.

Further, Augustine's view on marriage was influential throughout church history. Augustine focused on three goods of marriage: faithfulness, children, and sacrament. In addition, another good could be friendship. Aquinas shifted the language to the "ends" of marriage and created a hierarchy of ends. For Aquinas, the primary end was procreation, rather than union of the spouses. Scholars note that this choice assigns the priority to marriage for what was considered "animal nature" rather than "human nature."[8]

During this time, the consent of both partners created a marriage, not a ceremony. In northern Europe, marriage was consent followed by sexual intercourse. In the twelfth century, Canon Law combined these two perspectives to state that consent is the beginning of marriage and sexual intercourse completes the process of marriage. Betrothal (engagement) was the beginning of marriage. Then when sexual intercourse occurred, whether right away or after several years, the marriage process was completed. Premarital sex did not exist since people assumed sex for a couple was an act of marriage. Marriage was confirmed by the community when the woman became pregnant. For centuries, marriage was considered a process rather than signified by a single ceremonial starting event.

The Council of Trent changed this understanding, first stating that marriage was a sacrament. As a sacrament, it had to be celebrated with a priest and witnesses. Only then was a marriage valid. Marriage changed from a process completed over time to a single legal and sacramental event within the church.

Protestantism tried to rethink the notions of celibacy and marriage, to urge a positive view of marriage. In the Lutheran European context, marriage was part of God's plan for humans. Wives were to submit to their husbands in this partnership. Sex was allowed within marriage and the parents of the man and woman still arranged or agreed to the marriage. A gap remained between church teaching on the purpose of marriage and practice. Marriage was seen by most people as a practical way to have a stable life.

So where is the Christian tradition today? Within Catholicism, marriage unites one man and one woman for the purposes of procreation. The purpose of sex is to have children. Having sex also unites the couple. Anything that prohibits procreation is sinful. Masturbation is sinful; anal sex is sinful; oral sex is sinful. Any sex outside of marriage is sinful, even if it is to procreate. So the Catholic Church retained a focus on procreation, and within this focus, admitted that sexual desire can be good for the unity of the couple.

There are two important recent shifts within Catholic tradition. First, *Gaudium et Spes* ends the hierarchy of ends of marriage. Procreation is still important; however, so too is the union of the spouses. Second, Canon Law now states that "[t]he *matrimonial covenant*, by which a man and a woman establish between themselves a partnership of the whole of life, is by its nature ordered toward the good of the spouses and the procreation and education of offspring" (Code of Canon Law1055, 1). One could interpret this text to say that not every sexual act within marriage has to be open to procreation.

Within the Christian tradition as a whole, one finds three ways sex can be allowed. Sex can help bond a couple in marriage; sex can be an expression of the sacredness of marriage; sex can bring about children. These aspects of sexual relations within marriage have been respectively labeled the "unitive," the "sacramental," and the procreative. Hence, sexual intercourse can be celebrated within the bounds of marriage to differing extents. For example, Lutheranism and Anglicanism focus on what is known as commonwealth, marriage as the basis of society. The Reformed tradition emphasizes marriage as a covenant between two people and God.

Some theologians considered marriage in the context of community. Aelred,[9] for example, saw marriage as good for the couple and for the common good (Peterson, 33). It is possible to consider a relationship from the perspective of the whole community. What makes a relationship good in this context? In the biblical tradition, the aim was for procreation, to carry on a stable, ordered community. We may want to consider relationships differently now.

Understanding what makes a relationship "good" is critical not just for sex or marriage but for friendship too. Both Augustine and Aquinas argued that humans yearn for friendship with God. Friendships are also within the context of a community.

On Friendship

Since I argue that we should think about partnerships from the perspective of friendship, a note on friendship within the Christian tradition is important. This area is under-researched and underemphasized within the Christian tradition.

Aelred uses strong language for friendship, blurring the boundaries between a sexual and a nonsexual relationship. "It is no mean consolation in this life to have someone with whom you can be united by an intimate attachment and the embrace of very holy love, to have someone in whom your spirit may rest, to whom you can pour out your soul" (Aelred quoted in Quero 2004, 44). Here, he is speaking about his friendship with a male friend. He continues: "In the sleep of peace, you alone may repose with him alone in the embrace of charity, the kiss of unity, with the sweetness of the Holy Spirit flowing between you" (Aelred in Quero 2004, 44). The deep love in this relationship blurs the lines between agapic love and eros, both being present in this friendship.

Other scholars within Judaism and Christianity discuss friendship and relations between persons in this world. For example, Martin Buber[10] talks about I–Thou relationships. For Buber, we experience others but never fully. We are in ever-growing relationship with others, based on love.

Strands of the Christian tradition could be reread to better understand friendship. For example, Origen, a Greek theologian in the third century, talked about the important link between agape and eros, even in our love of friends. In my opinion, friendship does not have to include sexual acts but it could. The love of friends is enhanced both by agape and by eros.

Augustine noted one of the goods of marriage was friendship. For him, there is good in marriage, even if the couple remains childless. He also speaks of friendship in general. For Augustine, friendship is based on mutually wanting good for the other. Friends do not exist for our own ends. Instead, true friendship is mutual; my friend wants all good things for me and I want all good things for my friend. As friendships expand out to the community, they want good for the community as a whole.

Most within the Christian tradition have distinguished between friendship and marriage, seeing marriage as the basis of society. Yet, friendship could be so. Here we need to unpack some of the theology around love. As I noted in the chapter on desire, we wrongly assigned positivity to agape (disinterested love) and negativity to eros (deeply interested love). In friendships, all aspects of love are important and the Christian tradition needs to address this more fully.[11]

Theology

Theologically, then, I want to begin thinking about relationships without privileging marriage. Marriage has excluded many people and has not ensured good relationships within its boundaries. How might we structure good relationships?

Any relationship can stimulate and celebrate desire. An ethic of justice in relationships and in the wider community can bring us closer to knowing God. Our sexual relationships are part of building this wider community. As we build relationships with each other we come to know God. We need to know others to know God. Limiting our knowing to one person limits our ability to know God.

What if we considered the Trinity as a model for relationships? First of all, the Trinity shows us that three can be one; it does not have to be two. Further, the Trinity helps us understand the element of close communion. God, Jesus Christ, and the Holy Spirit are all aspects of God in close relation with each other. Marcella Althaus-Reid celebrates this Trinitarian love as "polyfidelity" (2003, 58–59). If we come to know God through knowing others, then we should know more than one other person intimately, to more fully be in relation with God.

A person can commit to relationships with more than one person. We know this as friendship; though we usually prohibit sex. Friendships connect us to God through the other. Developing relationships with others helps to develop faith. Loving others helps us to learn to love God. It helps us to love the world. Rather than seeing our love as limited to a partner, we should see this love as teaching us how to love fully and unconditionally. There is no limit to love. There is no reason why our friendships couldn't be sexual; all relationships can connect us to God when they are just.

The concept of commitment or covenant is important here. Covenant is committing to a relationship with particular intent and aims. God created a covenant with us and we can create covenants with each other. As we love others, we love God; as we get to know others we are knowing God. Sex can be part of this covenant in any relationship. This commitment sits within the wider community. We ignore this broader community at our peril if we think of a relationship as solely between two individuals. We all belong to God. We are all in community together and no one possesses another.

Structures should exist to support just relationships across the spectrum from platonic friendship to sexual relationships. For example, if we argue that sin is domination and exertion of power over another, then our laws and structures should support the sharing of power rather than domination. Sin exists in the lack of consent, mutuality, and honesty. Sin exists in the structures that prohibit us from knowing God. One such structure today is marriage.

Act

1. Stop privileging marriage. Two people could decide to enter a relationship for life and want to formalize this relationship through the church or the state. However, the focus on marriage as the primary space for sexual relationship must change. It is unjust and privileges the few over the many. Work toward changing structures that privilege marriage: taxes, hospital visitor regulations for emergency and intensive care, and so forth.
2. Rethink friendship as the basis for structures of relationship, your own friendships and others. Talk about what this shift would look like. What is good about any relationship is its mutuality and equality. The same is true for society. As we explore friendships through mutuality and honesty, pleasure is developed. This pleasure can extend to the world at large.
3. Rethink sexual partnerships. We need to be creative and open. Again, mutuality and equality are the basic elements for partnership. As we treat our partner(s) as fully human, we can learn to treat everyone as fully human. As we come to know each other, we come

to know God. We can extend this concept to all our relationships, realizing we are desirable as we desire others. Erotic desire can lead us to good.

4. Work to end racism, sexism, classism, and so forth. It will be much easier to form mutual partnerships when society itself is focused on equality. It will be much easier to celebrate desire and sex in this context.

Moving Forward

When we think of our sexual relationships, friendships, and partnerships, marriage may be an option but it is not necessarily the right or just option for many. Rather, we should insist that any partnership is mutual, consensual, and adds to the whole of the community. We can consider relationships and friendship more broadly, as well as how desire and sex can play a role within our relationships.

Finally, to point toward the last chapter, I want to address reproduction. People can have and raise children as part of a relationship. However, reproduction and child-rearing do not have to be linked to a sexual relationship. In biblical times, marriage was a way to ensure paternity. Sex led to pregnancy and the children had to be able to fit into a lineage. However, in our time, birth control exists. Childbearing and child-rearing may be part of a nonsexual relationship too. One can have a child without intercourse.

So, in sum, one is complete in God; one is not complete in a relationship, any relationship. In each of our relationships, with every human being, we should commit to honesty, mutuality, and justice.

Questions for Reflection

1. In terms of a sexual partnership, which is more important to you: friendship or marriage? Why?
2. Why do you think marriage remains an important cornerstone of some societies? Should it be?
3. Could you have "good" sex without marriage? Could you have "good" sex without friendship? Why or why not?

Further Suggested Readings

Abbott, Elizabeth. 2010. A History of Marriage: from same sex unions to private vows and common law, the surprising diversity of a tradition. New York: Seven Stories Press.

This excellent book traces the history of concepts of marriage and how they have been practiced differently throughout time and space. Abbot also addresses issues of race, class, sexuality, and laws with regard to marriage, connecting the history of these issues with their expressions in the marital context today.

Thatcher, "Framing Sex: Must the Framework Be Marriage?" In Thatcher, Adrian. 2011. God, Sex, and Gender: An Introduction. Malden: Wiley-Blackwell, 76–95.

Thatcher's chapter introduces arguments for supporting or rejecting marriage. His contexts include the historical strand of Christianity that prioritized celibacy and those that consider marriage within the context of justice or friendship.

Thorne, Gary. 2010. "Friendship: The End of Marriage," In Jeal, Roy R, ed. Human Sexuality and the Nuptial Mystery, 45–64. Eugene: Cascade Books.

Thorne's chapter is set within the debate over same-sex unions. However, within this context, he articulates the importance of both eros and agape in friendship. It is an excellent starting point for a much-needed reconsideration of friendship within the Christian tradition.

Notes

1. Ellison is a scholar and professor working in sexual ethics.
2. "In the Old Testament, adultery always means having sex with another man's wife or fiancée. It is a violation of the rights of the husband or fiancé. For a married man to have sex with an unmarried woman is viewed in Scripture as immoral, but it is not considered adultery, since it is a violation of the rights and dignity of the unmarried woman's father, not her husband (cf. Exod. 22:16–17; Deut. 22:28–29)" (Brownson 113–14, footnote).
3. Roeber's book is an excellent resource on the history of marriage.
4. "The National Coalition Against Domestic Violence provides some sobering statistics: in terms of adults, one in four women experiences domestic abuse during her lifetime; 85 percent of victims of intimate violence are women; and one in six women and one in thirty-three men have experienced rape, either attempted or completed. Moreover, forced sex or sexual assault occurs in approximately 45 percent of battering relationships" (Ellison 2012, 80).
5. "Nearly two-fifths of rape crimes are perpetrated within the presumed intimacy of heterosexual marriage" (Ellison 2012, 80).

6. See Nelson (1978) for an excellent analysis of fidelity and problems with the concept of marriage.
7. Luther (1483–1546) was a German theologian and former monk who argued against several aspects of the Roman Catholic Church of his time, helping to spawn the Protestant Reformation.
8. See, for example, Salzman and Lawler, 27.
9. Aelred of Rievaulx was an English monk and abbot, who lived from 1110 to 1167.
10. Buber, a Jewish philosopher, lived from 1878 to 1965.
11. This is slowly happening. See, for example, Thorne.

References

Abbott, Elizabeth. 2010. *A History of Marriage: From Same Sex Unions to Private Vows and Common Law, the Surprising Diversity of a Tradition.* New York: Seven Stories Press.

Althaus-Reid, Marcella. 2000. *Indecent Theology: Theological Perversions in Sex, Gender and Politics.* London: Routledge.

———. 2003. *The Queer God.* London: Routledge.

Browning, Melissa. 2014. *Risky Marriage: HIV and Intimate Relationships in Tanzania.* Lanham: Lexington Books.

Brownson, James. 2013. *Bible, Gender, Sexuality: Reframing the Church's Debate on Same-Sex Relationships.* Grand Rapids: William B. Eerdmans.

Code of Canon Law, *Marriage.* 1055, I. http://www.vatican.va/archive/ENG1104/_P3V.HTM

Ellison, Marvin. 2012. *Making Love Just: Sexual Ethics for Perplexing Times.* Minneapolis: Fortress Press.

Nelson, James. 1978. *Embodiment: An Approach to Sexuality and Christian Theology.* Minneapolis: Augsburg.

Peterson, Anna. 2009. *Everyday Ethics and Social Change: The Education of Desire.* New York: Columbia University Press.

Quero, M.H.C. 2004. Friendship with Benefits: A Queer Reading of Aelred of Rievaulx and His Theology of Friendship. In *The Sexual Theologian: Essays on Sex, God and Politics*, ed. Marcella Althaus-Reid and Lisa Isherwood, 26–46. London: T&T Clark.

Roeber, A.G. 2012. *Hopes for Better Spouses: Protestant Marriage and Church Renewal in Early Modern Europe, India, and North America.* Grand Rapids: Eerdmans.

Salzman, Todd A., and Michael G. Lawler. 2012. *Sexual Ethics: A Theological Introduction.* Washington, DC: Georgetown University Press.

Thatcher, Adrian. 2011a. *God, Sex, and Gender: An Introduction.* Malden: Wiley-Blackwell.

———. 2011b. Framing Sex: Must the Framework Be Marriage? In *God, Sex, and Gender: An Introduction*, ed. Adrian Thatcher, 76–95. Wiley-Blackwell: Malden.

Thorne, Gary. 2010. Friendship: The End of Marriage. In *Human Sexuality and the Nuptial Mystery*, ed. Roy R. Jeal, 45–64. Eugene: Cascade Books.

CHAPTER 5

Sex Work

Abstract Rejecting the Christian tradition's condemnation of sex work, this chapter considers how the sex trade could become just. It begins with a definition of sex work, explores the historical context around this work, and articulates how to reconsider sex work from the perspective of the workers, with reference to the biblical tradition, the Christian tradition, and theology.

Keywords Sex work • Prostitute • John • Sex trade • Decriminalization

The sex trade is considered to be the opposite end of the spectrum from marriage, usually condemned from an ethical perspective, though the sex trade fits comfortably in a capitalist society where generation of money is the focus. However, marriage can be seen as part of the sex trade, for example, when one pays a family a dowry in exchange for a wife or a marriage where a woman traded sex in exchange for economic support, or worse, marriage seen as property where the man owned the woman. Setting marriage aside for the moment and focusing on the formal trade in sex, I want to ask: Can there be mutual desire, pleasure, and knowing? We have already seen Jesus' lineage contains women who traded sex, so why is the sex trade condemned?

T. Cooper, *A Christian Guide to Liberating Desire, Sex, Partnership, Work, and Reproduction*,
https://doi.org/10.1007/978-3-319-70896-6_5

Sex and economics are linked. In individual relationships, one might "trade" sex for dinner and a movie, for taking care of the kids. In sex work, a prostitute trades sexual labor for money; labor is sold, not the body.

What does the sexual theology of those who buy and sell sex look like? From an economic and gender perspective I explore what leads people into the sexual marketplace, sex work in particular. Christian theology should not condemn sex work on moral grounds. Theology should condemn the racist, sexist, heterosexist economic system, exploiting people working in the sex industry. Labeling prostitution morally wrong worsens the situation of people who work with selling sex. Moral condemnation amplifies the disparaging treatment of sex workers. If we celebrate sex as a way to know God, we could work toward a fair sex trade. Having seen good desire, good sex, and good relationship, now let's ask whether these can exist in the sex industry.

Definition

Sex work is the exchange of sexual acts for payment. There are three important qualifications. First, the body is not sold; that is slavery. Instead, the labor of sex is bought and sold. Thus, in sex work, a person uses the body to work. The body continues to belong to God.

Second, the sexual acts include more than intercourse. "I pamper them and … I also give them a really good massage which includes the feet and the head … in addition to any of the more overt sexual practice, there is the touching and holding and the caressing the cuddling and sometimes bathing together" (Gayle qtd in Ipsen, 143). Sex, companionship, and intimacy are all exchanged.

Third, sex work expands beyond the formal sex trade. However, we will begin with the formal selling and buying of sex.

Historical Context

Prostitution has been called the oldest trade. We have several examples in the biblical text, as in other sacred texts. The introduction explored Jesus' genealogy as one example. Prostitution itself was never fully accepted but women who sold sex have been celebrated for actions they took in the course of their work. We know that even priests made use of prostitutes.

Throughout history, sex work was condemned or tolerated depending on the context. To take just one example, when syphilis spread throughout the European continent in the late 1400s and early 1500s, there was a crackdown on prostitution. In 1521, the king of Portugal exiled prostitutes from Lisbon. Prostitutes were blamed for spreading the disease, though we know that the male colonizers themselves brought it to the Americas, where it devastated the native population.

When the male conquistadors invaded, they arrived without families and had sex with indigenous women. This "trade" in sex enabled some indigenous individuals to survive. However, the colonizers had power over the indigenous people. Further, women were a commodity exchanged between men. The Christian tradition supported this economic system. The men did not marry the indigenous women. The children born in this context could be part of a colonial society; the indigenous women could not.

Some people living in the colonies worked against the marginalization of the indigenous. In Brazil, for example, Jesuits suggested Portuguese prostitutes be brought to Brazil. The Jesuits argued that this would lessen the exploitation of native women and perhaps improve the situation of women-excluded Portuguese society. The sex work was transferred from slaves to European women.

Prostitutes and other women were not often differentiated, whether European or native. All women were treated as the sexual property of men. By the end of the sixteenth century, the Inquisition arrived in Brazil. Sex was on its agenda. The Inquisitors condemned same-sex relations for men and for women but did not attend to either prostitution or adultery. The priority was solely to ensure sexual acts could lead to procreation. I will address the Christian tradition further in a later section.

Sex work continues unabated today, though illegal in most countries. Sex tourism invites wealthy travelers to poorer countries to have sex. Every country has sex to sell. In addition, women are often trafficked from other countries to the USA to serve in the sex trade. US citizens also work in the trade.

Hermeneutical Circle

See

Selling Sex

Our conversation will be primarily in communities with people who sell sex. From a liberationist perspective, priority should be given to those with the least power. In our economic system, we need to work to live. Yet, it is also a choice: to survive, to support a family, or to develop a career.

Important here is the power to choose, which is determined by economics, race, gender, and sexuality.

The first step is to enter sex work. Since sex is exchanged for money, there is a financial rationale. Once a person enters sex work, the question is to what extent she/he can say no in any given situation. Forced sex is rape. Consent is important. The next step is to set limits on the sex acts. The third step is usually to extend those boundaries. A final step is exiting the industry. All of these choices are constrained by the worker's economic, racial, and other situations. If she/he has no money, there is less choice; she/he may risk disease or death. If she/he has to work on the street, she/he may face more violence. In society, this inequality of power can be due to economic, racial, sexual, and other components based on our history of slavery, marginalization of women and people of color, religious discrimination, and so forth.

Purchasing Sex

The buyer in the sex trade is often overlooked both within the Christian tradition and in society in general. However, one could not sell sex without a buyer. Most literature portrays consumers negatively but detailed research is needed. One buys sex for several reasons: (1) mainly male, he may not have access to sex; (2) he may want to have sex whenever he wants; (3) he may want to avoid relationships; (4) he may enjoy secrecy; (5) he may explore particular desires; (6) he may want to feel loved; (7) he may want to have a particular sexual experience; (8) he may be lonely or shy. The market for sex is diverse, though mainly geared toward men. Women too occasionally pay for sex.

Managing Sex

There are often managers of sex work: pimps, protectors, or brothel owners. Is management positive or negative for the sex worker? There is little analysis of "pimps." Rita Nakashima Brock and Susan Thistlethwaite,[1] for example, argue that pimps most likely come from abusive families, but they acknowledge the lack of actual research.[2] A pimp is a manager, similar to any manager within the capitalist system. This go-between can give the sex worker more choice or can take choice away.

So we have identified at least some of the groups in the community who can reflect. Now academic tools can help us to analyze the situation. If we eradicated gender, racial, economic, and sexual inequality, who would buy, manage, and sell sex?

Judge

Academics

I analyzed capitalism in previous chapters. From an economic standpoint, one may conclude that sex work is not different from the exploitation that takes place through capitalism's focus on wage labor. The sex trade grows the economy. Sex is a commodity. Alternatives to capitalism, focused on equality rather than profit, could make labor (including sex) more just.

The economy also often causes increased sex work due to its negative effects in terms of "economic growth." As rural people lose land and need to move to the cities, prostitution increases. As people fall into debt, prostitution increases. Colonization, war, and other disruptions also cause a rise in prostitution. Sex work increases when people are removed from their normal means for survival. Maria Mies, a German feminist sociologist, labeled the International Monetary Fund (IMF) and the World Bank the "International of Pimps" because their focus on International Division of Labor has caused sex tourism to grow. In our capitalist economy, the sex trade is a way to increase economic growth.

In some cases, this combination of prohibition and encouragement leads to sex trafficking. There is relatively free movement of money around the world but not labor. In order to move labor, people are trafficked, illegally taken out of and brought into countries, often bought and sold. The economic system encourages these sex "corporations" to exploit individuals. People caught are punished but the vast majority are still able to participate in the market. The size of the sex trade and its slavery/trafficking component suggest the huge economic gains outweigh the illegality.

However, from the perspective of some sex workers, prostitution can be a way of taking charge of one one's situation, gaining some control. For example, one Indian study showed women selling sex feel more in charge economically and feel less constricted by social norms. Anagha Tambe[3] argues that, in the Indian context, women are expected to repress their sexual desires (2008). Because true equality in sexual relationships seems a fantasy, female sex worker organizations articulate sex work as a means toward equality. In particular, these organizations do not critique men for purchasing sex. The purchase of sex is simply an effect of the prevailing society. Some see sex work as a way to maintain honesty in a sexual relationship in an unjust world. The sex workers in Ipsen's research agree. More research needs to be done here.

Gender discrimination is bound within this capitalist system. Even feminists tend to disparage women who sell sex, labeling sex workers either as victims or as morally wrong. Instead, we all would benefit from thinking about sex work as a form of labor, with its economically exploitative and patriarchal underpinnings.

Intersectionality: Gender, Race, and Sexuality

Women suffer from economic disparity with men and from patriarchy. Patriarchy is the situation in our society where men remain atop the hierarchy. Mainly, women sell sex to men. The sex market is mainly geared toward male desire. Would the sex trade become more just if this changed? Further, as we've asked before, can any exchange of sex be mutual in our patriarchal society?

Beyond this analysis, the perspectives of transpeople need to be brought into the conversation. Gender and sex are along a spectrum. Transpeople, for example, are overrepresented in the sex trade because society discriminates against them. Other types of discrimination increase this overrepresentation. For example, 47% of transgender African-Americans report they have engaged in sex work (Scholl, 45).

Further, white people disproportionately purchase sex and people of color disproportionately sell sex. This inequality mirrors the history of people of color being used as commodities by white people. One study showed that while women of color are 40% of prostitutes working on the streets in the USA, they are 85% of those arrested, convicted, and sent to jail (Brock & Thistlethwaite, 152). We need to pay attention to the intersection of race, class, and sex.

There is also a hierarchy of sexuality in the sex trade, with the main focus on the heterosexual market. Yet, the denigration of homosexuality, bisexuality, and so forth in society means the sex trade can be a place to express sexuality in secret. And people who are not "heterosexual" can also be excluded from other workplaces, leaving sex work as one option. This area is also under-researched.

Our choice of where and how to labor is limited by these oppressions. Individuals cannot always choose if and when to enter the sex market, and whether and when to have sex. Apart from the oppressions explored earlier, people may also be marginalized due to age, nationality, religion, physical and mental health, and so forth.

What would the exchange of sex look like without these varying oppressions? People would sell and buy sex depending on the particular skill or exchange desired, free of constraints.

Politics

Politically, there are four approaches to sex work: abolition, prohibition, regulation, and decriminalization. The prevalent aim for most people, including feminists, is abolition: the end of the sex trade. This perspective tends to view sex workers as victims. This view influences international and national laws, arguing that sex work is inherently abusive, that no person would choose to trade sex for money. Yet many sex workers argue that abolition does nothing to stop the exploitation some workers face. Rescuing someone from the industry opens a place for another to enter.

The second aim, often used alongside the first, is prohibition. Prohibition criminalizes sex work. In this view, a sex worker is a criminal (and possibly a victim as well) and should be punished or rehabilitated. Prohibition takes power away from the sex worker, since all legal avenues for redress of any bad situation are blocked. Instead, the sex worker herself is in danger of being arrested. In this system, often, workers need pimps or managers to have any means of protection.

The third approach is legalization. While legalization does not criminalize sex work, there are several negatives. For example, legalization requires a sex worker to officially register. In our society, where sex workers are marginalized, stating sex work as one's occupation can reduce the chances of ever being hired for another job. Sex workers may avoid this marginalization, lacking power by not being registered. Further, the legalization may be temporary, creating a register of sex workers that could be used against them later on. A similar example is the Dream Act (DACA), which under the Obama administration enabled some undocumented youth to attain permission to temporarily reside in the USA. Under the Trump administration, this list of Dreamers is now under threat and the documentation may be used to deport them. Migrants without documents, who did not participate in DACA, can remain somewhat under the radar.

In contrast to legalization, most sex workers prefer decriminalization. Decriminalization means no longer making sex work illegal. Sex work is neither regulated nor criminalized. Sex workers can exercise their rights and protections without fear. As we work toward a more just system, where people in the sex trade are not exploited, decriminalization is a good start. Decriminalization helps sex workers access laws already in place: laws against murder, assault, blackmail, child abuse, and so on.

We also need to remember noncitizen sex workers. Marginalized due to lack of proper documentation, people are more likely to be drawn into sex work. Once there, they have no access to the rights and protections a citizen would have. Decriminalization would help to reduce harm against sex workers. However, we still live in a society where men exercise power over women, whites exercise power over people of other races, and citizens exercise power over noncitizens.

Due to these oppressions, Belliotti argues, "full social equality must be a prerequisite for mutuality" (118). We need to end capitalism, racism, sexism, and heterosexism at a structural level. Then, I argue, individuals could buy and sell sex depending on the particular skill or exchange desired, unconstrained by these exploitative structures and practices.

Let's explore what faith can add to the conversation.

Bible

There are many biblical texts including some "trade" in sex. As Abraham and Sarah migrated, Abraham offered Sarah to others (Gen. 20). Ruth used her sexuality to gain a place in Boaz' household (see esp. Ruth 3). William Loader notes biblical law never specifically prohibited sex with prostitutes (Loader 2012, 15). However, New Testament writers speak out against prostitution, though several "sex workers" form Jesus' lineage, as the introduction explained.

One can read the biblical text as supportive of sex workers. Avaren Ipsen[4] read texts in community with sex workers. Reading the story of Rahab (Joshua 2, 6:22–25), the sex workers emphasized that Rahab had agency. She chose to do sex work. She sacrificed her body for her family.[5] Within the Jewish tradition, Rahab is an important and respected woman, with kings and others in her lineage.[6] So the sex worker reading has parallels in aspects of Judaism.

Another scripture often read in the context of prostitution appears in all four Gospels: the Anointing Woman.[7] Within the Christian tradition, the woman who pours ointment on Jesus' head and feet is alternately deemed a repentant prostitute or not a prostitute. The sex workers reading with Ipsen state that the denial of her as a prostitute excludes the fact that much of the work of sex is not intercourse. There is massaging, pampering, and so forth. Further, the sex workers reject the label of "sinner" applied to her. If she was a sinner, it was not due to sex work.

Christian Tradition

The Christian tradition's response to prostitution has included toleration, prohibition, and an aim for abolition. Christianity moved from tolerating prostitution to condemning women for tempting men, to seeing sex workers as victims needing rescue.

Priestly celibacy was not always enforced within Roman Catholicism. In the Middle Ages, for example, some priests married and many others had mistresses. When the church began to emphasize priestly celibacy in the twelfth century, some kings added a tax on priests for having sex.[8] Men sinned by not controlling their desires. Eve was blamed for the sin in the garden; however, prostitutes were simply following her lead. The man should control his desire; women were considered too weak to do so.

After the Reformation, theologians condemned both sex work and the women involved. Luther argued thus: "Through special enemies of our faith, the devil has sent some whores here to ruin our poor young men. … As an old and faithful preacher I ask you in fatherly fashion, dear children, that you believe assuredly that the evil spirit sent these whores here and that they are dreadful, shabby, stinking, loathsome, and syphilitic, as daily experience unfortunately demonstrates" (Luther qtd. in Brock and Thistlethwaite, 133). Where, previously, the women were seen as simply responding to male desires, this perspective had shifted. Women became the sinners.

Over time the church has viewed sex workers as weak women, sinners, and victims. Christian churches today tend to welcome the repentant ex–sex worker. Many Christians still condemn the work. Rarely do the churches examine the structures of sin; they still focus on the notion that having sex outside of marriage is sinful.

Theology

Liberation theology, in contrast, focuses on naming and working against structural sin. Racism, sexism, classism, and heterosexism are sinful. For just sex, we must eradicate structural sin.

First, theology should begin from sex worker perspectives. Rose Wu, a theologian and activist, suggests theology must "allow prostitutes to reclaim, redefine, rename and recreate their sacredness and wholeness that is the gift of God to everyone" (80). Liberation theology begins from the perspective of the marginalized, the poor. "The whole climate of the

Gospel is a continual demand for the right of the poor to make themselves heard, to be considered preferentially by society, a demand to subordinate the economic needs to those of the deprived" (Gutierrez 1974, 116) In this case, the deprived are the sex workers.

Second, sex workers also critique the focus on individual sin. The wider society is unjust, not the act of sex. The sin is in the exploitation. Calling on sex workers to repent ignores the unjust structures constraining their choices.

For these sex workers, the entire system is to blame, not the men and women who purchase and sell sex. Ipsen argues that we need more research into "exceptional insider" stories, stories of men who empathize with sex workers and work with them for justice. This research could happen more easily without the stigma attached to buying and selling sex. Buyers and sellers can both work to make the trade of sex more just.

Ipsen also considers sex work in terms of sacrifice. Why blame the prostitute when she is working to support herself and others? She asks why the sacrifice of Jesus' body is considered noble but the sacrifice of women's bodies is not. If one can argue that Jesus sacrificed himself for others, why could one not argue the same for prostitutes? Once the sex is acknowledged as good rather than sinful, why the shame in prostitution?

So how could we counter the condemnation of sex and sex work? Ipsen and the sex workers in her group argue that "God is not opposed to sex per se but rather it is domination, coercion, and exploitation that offend whatever divinity they pray to" (150). Indeed, sex is a way to know God. Sex work could be sacred. Any just exchange of sex can be a way to know God.

As argued earlier, liberation theologians say we come to know God through knowing others. Sin is when injustice enters that relation. If I treat you unjustly, then I am treating God unjustly. What I do unto you, I do "unto Christ." All relationships have this potential for inequality, including sexual relationships. Jesus is the sex worker trying to support her family. How can we make the exchange mutual?

Any exchange, whether part of the sex trade or the economy in general, is either just or unjust. According to Enrique Dussel, an Argentinian philosopher, "when a shoemaker exchanges shoes for bread, a relationship between persons arises" (1988, 79). If the trade is mutually beneficial, then the relationship is just. However, if I am out to get the best deal I can, the other person becomes an object. This usage is encouraged by structures. In our structures of sin, we are forced into unjust relationships, whether we want to be or not. A just economy would focus on human well-being rather than on profit.

In a just sex trade, each person would come to the table freely and be treated fairly.

Act

So from the perspective of the sex workers, how could we move forward? First, each of the suggestions from the previous chapters holds true here. Sexual desire is positive when power is shared and there is consent. Sex is also positive under these conditions.

1. Minimize harm to sex workers. We should work alongside the sellers, buyers, and managers of sex to counter the harmful sexist, racist, heterosexist, and classist aspects of the sexual marketplace. Consent is critical to the sex trade. One must have the choice to say no to sex. Rape occurs in the sex trade. Any time one is forced to have sex, that is rape. There is a sliding scale of consent. A sex worker may be able to refuse a particular act but may need to work in the trade. Here, agency is important: the extent to which a person can make choices. For example, if you are trafficked, you have no agency. Addiction and poverty can take away agency. However, many sex workers do have agency. They choose the work to support themselves or their family. For example, the work offers flexible hours so one can be at home with children when needed.

   In a previous article, I suggested the following for a fairer sex trade, based on the model of fair trade: "1. Be organized democratically by the sellers; 2. Have sex worker unions; 3. Have sellers and buyers of legal age; 4. Have 'decent working conditions'; 5. Not damage the environment; 6. Ensure sex workers were paid a fair wage; 7. Ensure sex workers were paid enough to continue improving their conditions; 8. Ensure that buyers and sellers would build long-term relationships" (Cooper 2011, 205–06). Minimizing harm must sit alongside working to change our systems.
2. Decriminalize sex work. Most often sex workers want the trade to be decriminalized. Sex workers want to be protected by existing laws: laws against rape, exploitative labor, and so forth. Sex workers want to be recognized as full human beings. We also need to apply these laws to people who are trafficked. One example of improving

the lives of sex workers comes from the Latin American continent. Since the 1970s, sex worker unions have aimed to make the process fairer. By creating a labor union, abuses can be redressed under labor laws.

3. Work to end racism, sexism, heterosexism, classism. Our unjust system causes more people to be in sex work than who want to be. We need to change this system. We need to work toward alternatives to capitalism and end racism, sexism, and heterosexism. This action is critical for each of our chapters.

   Unfortunately, many studies tend to focus on the individual sex worker rather than on the system. While it is important for an individual to have choice, many other societal factors need to be taken into account, for example, male domination of women and so forth. As we know, sex today exists in a patriarchal system. Sex is influenced by economics, politics, race, and so forth. How then could we move from decriminalization to a just sex work system? The sex worker would choose to do this work, not do it from economic necessity. She/he would choose when and how to do this work and with whom to have sex. Others would see her as a worker, not as a victim or criminal.

Moving Forward

Sex can be a way to know God, even within the sex trade. In our system of exploitation due to race, class, sex, and sexuality, however, much sex is unjust. To work toward justice, we should

1. Encourage Christians and Christian churches to support, rather than blame, sex workers and instead address structures of sin.
2. Work toward justice with sex workers.
3. Advocate for decriminalization of the sex trade.
4. Work to minimize the violence and harm within the sex trade.
5. Acknowledge that the sex trade is only one example of our unjust system.
6. Celebrate sex as a way to know God.

Questions for Reflection

1. Do you think it is possible to have fairly traded sex? Why or why not?
2. Could sex work include "good" sex? Why or why not?
3. I suggested at the beginning of the chapter that sex work and marriage could be considered on a similar spectrum. Having read the chapter on partnership and this one on sex work, what is your perspective?

Further Suggested Reading

Brock, Rita Nakashima, and Susan Thistlethwaite. 1996. *Casting Stones: Prostitution and Liberation in Asia and the United States.* Minneapolis: Augsburg Fortress.

This seminal text on sex work analyzes the situation from an international perspective, contextualizing the trade in the USA and East Asia. Critical of the trade in sex, they are also critical of the typical Christian response of blaming the sex worker. This book argues for a shift in the way communities respond to the trade in sex, suggesting an approach of solidarity to end the trade.

Ipsen, A. 2009. *Sex Working and the Bible.* London: Equinox.

Ipsen's book engages sex workers in a reading of biblical texts from Rahab to the Whore of Babylon. It is an excellent mix of an analysis from a liberationist perspective on sex work and, most importantly, an analysis from sex workers themselves, who do not argue for the end of the sex trade but for a fairer working situation.

Wu, Rose. 2001. "Women on the Boundary: Prostitution, Contemporary and in the Bible," *Feminist Theology*, 28, 69–81.

Wu's article argues for a theological shift with regard to sex work. This shift begins not with dogma but with listening to the voices of sex workers themselves, to understand the complex context of their own theologies of sex work.

Notes

1. Brock is an author, minister, and director of Faith Voices for the Common Good. Thistlethwaite is a professor of theology at Chicago Theological Seminary.
2. "Pimp behavior suggests that they are trained for the job in abusive families. ... *We say "suggests" because, as far as we can determine, little formal research has been done on the psychology of pimps*" (162–63; Italics mine).

3. Tambe is a sociologist at the Center for Women's Studies, University of Pune, India.
4. Ipsen has a Ph.D. in Biblical Literature and has lectured at UC Berkeley in Interdisciplinary Studies.
5. They interpreted Rahab as "always an agent, despite whatever constraints impinge on her decisions. Rahab chose to do sex work to make a living to help her family. … Sacrifice for family, even when it is a sacrifice that many respectable people cannot imagine opting for, needs to be recognized even if an utterly different kind of economy that does not require such sacrifice is desirable and needs to be envisioned" (Ipsen, 85).
6. "included along with Noah's wife, Sarah, Rebekah, Leah, Rachel, Miriam, Hannah, Naomi, Ruth and Esther as a woman of valor. … Among her descendants were seven kings, along with numerous priests and prophets, including Jeremiah, Baruch, Ezekiel, and Huldah" (Guider, 30).
7. Matthew 26:6–13; Mark 14:3–9; Luke 7:36–50; John 12:1–8.
8. To give just one example, "The city of Toulouse used the tax on prostitutes to build the university" (Brock and Thistlethwaite, 104).

References

Belliotti, Raymond. 1993. *Good Sex: Perspectives on Sexual Ethics.* Lawrence: University Press of Kansas.

Brock, Rita Nakashima, and Susan Thistlethwaite. 1996. *Casting Stones: Prostitution and Liberation in Asia and the United States.* Minneapolis: Augsburg Fortress.

Cooper, Thia. 2011. Fair Trade Sex: Reflections on God, Sex, and Economics. *Feminist Theology* 19: 194–207.

Dussel, Enrique. 1988. *Ethics and Community.* Maryknoll: Orbis Books.

Guider, Margaret Eletta. 1995. *Daughters of Rahab: Prostitution and the Church of Liberation in Brazil.* Minneapolis: Fortress Press.

Gutierrez, Gustavo. 1974. *A Theology of Liberation: History, Politics and Salvation.* London: SCM Press.

Ipsen, A. 2009. *Sex Working and the Bible.* London: Equinox.

Loader, William. 2012. *The New Testament on Sexuality.* Grand Rapids: Eerdmans.

Scholl, Lia Claire. 2012. *I Heart Sex Workers: A Christian Response to People in the Sex Trade.* St. Louis: Chalice Press.

Tambe, Anagha. 2008. Different Issues/Different Voices: Organization of Women in Prostitution in India. In *Prostitution and Beyond: An Analysis of Sex Work in India*, ed. Rohini Sahni, V. Kalyan Shankar, and Hemant Apte, 73–97. Thousand Oaks: Sage.

Wu, Rose. 2001. Women on the Boundary: Prostitution, Contemporary and in the Bible. *Feminist Theology* 28: 69–81.

CHAPTER 6

Reproduction

Abstract This chapter works toward a holistic theology of reproduction, considering issues of abortion, contraception, IVF, surrogacy, fetal selection, and sterilization. Arguing that reproduction should be considered in community, rather than in the context of a sexual relationship, this chapter articulates the situation of reproductive injustice and how one can work toward reproductive justice. Beginning with a definition of reproduction, it considers the historical and modern-day injustice for poor women and women of color, and through the Bible, tradition, and theology argues that reproduction should be framed within a theology of relatedness.

Keywords Reproduction • Abortion • Contraception • Procreation • Pregnancy

Many of the rules regarding sex and marriage aimed to ensure orderly reproduction through male lineage. The Catholic Church argued that procreation is the main purpose for sex. Today, many people can access reproductive technology, separating sex and sexual relationships from reproduction. We will assess reproduction in terms of justice and right relations. One can have a child without having sex and one can have sex without having a child.

Due to the history of the oppression of women and of women of color in particular, reproduction has many nuances. I address seven intersecting

T. Cooper, *A Christian Guide to Liberating Desire, Sex, Partnership, Work, and Reproduction*,
https://doi.org/10.1007/978-3-319-70896-6_6

issues briefly here: abortion, fetal selection, sterilization, childcare, surrogacy, in vitro fertilization (IVF), and contraception. We need to address these pieces together for several reasons. For example, in the USA, black women have abortions at three times the rate of white women but are less likely to be pro-choice.[1] One-third of women in the USA will get an abortion during their life. In our conversation about reproduction, I will focus on those most marginalized. Here, it is women of color. To take one example, "Marie Big Pipe … [a young mother] was incarcerated on a felony charge of 'assault with intent to commit serious bodily harm' because she breastfed her child while under the influence of alcohol. She was denied services to treat her substance abuse problem and access to abortion services when she became pregnant" (Smith[2] 2005, 126). Taking into account these situations, let us begin.

Definition

By reproduction I mean the bringing of children into the world. There are two areas: having children and preventing children. In terms of having children, we will consider surrogacy, IVF, and fetal selection. In terms of preventing children, we will consider abortion, contraception, and sterilization. Further, childcare is the result of reproduction.

Historical Context

During biblical times, sex was for procreation and contraception did not exist. The fetus was considered a child after quickening in the fourth month, when fetal movement was felt by the mother. Throughout history, and still today, male children were prioritized. Female children and children with disabilities could be killed, "thrown to the wolves." Abortion and infanticide occurred within both Greek and Roman cultures.

Further, women's menstruation has been considered problematic throughout history; menstruation made a woman impure. In the nineteenth century, the understanding of menstruation shifted from impurity to a medical disability. Rather than a natural process around fertility, menstruation was seen as disabling. Women were subject to the uncontrollable process of bleeding. Men were unaffected by this disability. Rather than women's bodies being seen as a positive place of fertility, the focus on menstruation as negative made women's bodies disabled.

The nineteenth century introduced a focus on health. Male bodies were considered inherently healthier. Further, health was often focused around issues of sex. Health care also focused on controlling the reproduction of people considered less desirable. Healthy wealthy white people should procreate. Others should not. Lack of desirability was related to race, sex, religion, ability, and class. Procreation must be considered from this historical perspective.

In more recent history, the ability to control pregnancy through abortion and contraception is laden with this perspective. As abortion became more accessible and slightly less dangerous at the turn of the century, it also became more controversial. Should white middle-class and wealthy women abort? Don't we want them to have children? The same questions surrounded the emergence of condoms and the birth control pill. These questions did not surround IVF and other technologies to produce children as they were limited to the wealthier classes, already encouraged to procreate.

I'll separate recent history into two sections, one on women of color and a brief one on white women, to illustrate the differing experiences of women around reproduction. Throughout US history, white women, particularly middle- and upper-class women, were encouraged to bear children. During colonial times, abortion was legal before quickening; however by the 1800s, abortion for white women was considered "race suicide."[3] White women were to reproduce the white race. This encouragement continued throughout the next century.

Culminating in Roe versus Wade, many white women argued they should have legal access to abortion. Until the 1970s, pregnant white middle-class women either had to bear the child or face an illegal abortion. In addition, white women had a difficult time accessing sterilization. Many doctors followed the rule that white women could only be sterilized if the woman's age multiplied by the number of children she had was 120 or above (Nelson, 75). This rule did not apply to men.

The medicalization of reproduction was closely tied to eugenics, at the turn of the century. The concept of blood and bloodlines was important. Racism became biologized (though we know there is more genetic variation within any racial category than between the social categories created). Protecting the purity of bloodlines became a rationale for reproductive control. This purity of blood extended to ability, sexuality, and class. Many people were categorized as "defective." To take two brief examples, black men were deemed sexual beasts, unable to control their sexuality. Disabled men too were thought to have uncontrolled sexuality. White women needed to be protected from these sexual threats. Disabled men and men of color were sterilized, often without their consent. In another form of "protecting" the "defective," people with disabilities were categorized as vulnerable. Because they could not resist predators, disabled people should be protected through sterilization. Finally, homosexuals were also deemed "defective." While homosexuals would not reproduce through heterosexual sex, they could seduce others into becoming homosexual. Or, pretending to be heterosexual, they could pass on their "defective" genes through reproduction.

Women of color in particular faced reproductive injustice. Throughout US history, little reproductive choice existed for women of color. During slavery, black women had to produce children to increase the numbers of slaves. Having and raising children was a horrifying experience for black women. Masters threatened to, and often did, sell the children. Further, black women had to submit to white male sexual urges without resistance. After slavery, black women were not to have children. For example, in the 1930s several states created and funded clinics to provide birth control to black women to reduce the black population (Nelson, 4).[4] Population control extended beyond black women to other women of color. When sterilization was legalized in Puerto Rico in 1937, it became the most heavily promoted contraception method.

Reproductive restrictions continued through the century. In the 1960s and 1970s, 13 states[5] proposed sterilization laws for women, aimed at lower numbers of children for single mothers and the poor. In Puerto Rico, the birth control pill was tested on women, resulting in several deaths in the 1960s. On the mainland, evidence of forced sterilizations grew. The best-selling *Our Bodies, Our Selves* talks about the "Mississippi Appendectomy," where black women were sterilized without their knowledge. Women were sterilized at the same time as giving birth or when having unrelated surgery. This forced sterilization was also true for other women of color. The Indian Health Service sterilized more than 25% of tribal women in the 1970s.[6] By the 1970s, Puerto Rican women in New York City were sterilized at more than seven times the numbers of white women.

Some people of color asked whether contraception was an encouragement for genocide. While this notion may seem paranoid, it was revealed in 1972 that the US Public Health Service had conducted research experiments on syphilitic black men in Tuskegee, Alabama, leaving their condition untreated (Nelson, 87), just one example of racism within the health system. Men in the Black Nationalist movements argued that birth control without accessible health care for women was harmful.

New contraceptives were also tested on women of color. In the 1980s, the USA held a Public Board of Inquiry as to whether Depo-Provera (DP), an injected contraceptive, was safe to use. The Inquiry concluded it was unsafe. However, from 1972 to 1978, a birth control clinic in Atlanta, Georgia, had given injections of DP to 9000 women of color for free, as part of DP's clinical trials. Patients were not told the drug lacked approval from the Food and Drug Administration (FDA). Further, while injections were free, removing the contraceptive due to negative side effects cost money. Judges also offered DP to women convicted of drug charges as an alternative to prison. This use without approval or explanation was also true abroad. In Namibia, for example, a doctor reported that women were routinely injected with contraceptives without being told.

Access to and enforcement of reproductive technologies is racist and classist. White women are prioritized over women of color and wealthy women over poor women. Due to economic and gender-based constraints, women often cannot choose whether to have sex or when having sex whether to use contraception. Further, even as women raise their economic or social status, they still may lack access to the resources they need for fertility control.

According to the Christian tradition, women should procreate. However, women of color are held to a double standard. I will tease out this double standard further with regard to seven reproduction issues in the following section.

Hermeneutical Circle

See

Preventing Childbirth: Abortion, Contraception, and Sterilization

I begin with abortion, the most controversial issue around reproduction. In the USA, abortion is legal during the first two trimesters of pregnancy. However, there is a lack of access. For example, Amnesty International criticizes the lack of federal funding for abortion, which impacts poor women, the military, and Native Americans using the Indian Health Service.

In addition, abortion services exist in only 13% of US counties (Jones and Kooistra, 46). So women need access to money and transportation in order to choose this option. Globally, women also struggle with access to abortion services.[7]

In addition, there are economic constraints. Economic constraints may mean a mother cannot provide for the children she already has if she has another.[8] In one study, 86% of black women having multiple abortions already had at least one child. Sixty-five percent of black women having their first abortion already had at least one child. For white women, the figures were 57% and 53% respectively. First, previous motherhood means one has to consider abortion seriously if one becomes pregnant. Can one support another child? Further, race intensifies this question.[9] Black women are often the main breadwinners in a family. Hence, black women must take into consideration the cost (economic, emotional, physical, etc.) of having another child. Studies show women who bear several children, particularly with children born close together, often suffer negative effects. Many women are aware of the need to choose between lives rather than choose life.

In many countries, abortion is illegal except in cases of rape or the endangerment of the mother's health. There is inequality in access to health care, endangering marginalized women more so than others. Further, although a woman who is raped clearly did not choose to become pregnant, proving rape in order to get an abortion can be difficult.

Contraception too is fraught with inequalities. Women have the main responsibility to prevent pregnancy. In many cultures, men refuse to use condoms. So women suffer both the expense and the health risks of preventing pregnancy. In addition, women do not always have the power to refuse sex.

One permanent form of contraception is sterilization. This issue is resonant today. In 2013, the UK High Court ordered that a man with learning disabilities is to be sterilized.[10] Forced sterilization is less common today in the USA; however, sterilization has been offered as an alternative to jail time. Further, some courts have ordered men and women not to have any more children for a certain period of time.[11]

Fetus Selection: Having and Preventing Children

Access to abortion can also be detrimental to marginalized groups. In societies where raising female children or children with disabilities is costly or where being female or disabled is seen as an obstacle to living a full life, one may "de-select" a female fetus or a fetus with a disability. One can also try to create a child with particular genetic characteristics, selecting or deselecting a fetus based on the characteristics a parent desires.

Encouraging Childbirth: IVF and Surrogacy

Reproduction includes the attempt to have a child. Infertility treatment is expensive, and not usually covered by insurance. While the vast majority of IVF treatments go to wealthy women due to the cost, women of color and poor women have lower fertility rates than wealthy and white women (Rubin and Phillips, 179).

This inequality is also the case with surrogacy. Wealthy white women hire women of color and poor women as surrogates. Wealthy US and European women also hire surrogates from poorer countries. For example, the surrogacy business in India has expanded rapidly over the past ten years. Wealthy women pay poor women in India and other parts of the world to bear children (Norsworthy et al., 68).

Inequalities exist throughout reproductive issues.

Judge

Academics

What constraints do women face in the decision-making process? Each woman should have control over her own reproduction; it is her right. However, contexts decide what choices women have. Laws constrain choice. Social constraints determine the norms of a community. Racism, classism, sexism, and so on constrain choice. We tend to say a woman can choose whether or not to have a child. However, women may not have access to medical resources, a woman may be under the control of another person, and her wider community may not enable her to make decisions.

Further, the choice is often about which lives to prioritize, not whether to choose life. Former President Barack Obama, when campaigning, was asked when a baby had human rights. Rick Warren, the interviewer, wanted to know "Why should unborn human life *not* be treated with the same dignity and respect that the rest of us consider is our due?" (Goldkamp, 81). This question leads me to ask: who are "the rest of us?" More than half the globe's population is forced to live on less than $1 per day.

Pro-choice rhetoric does not appeal to many women of color and poor women. Articulating abortion in terms of choice implies women have more than one choice and rests on many assumptions. The pro-life movement does not resonate either. Arguing from a pro-life perspective seems hypocritical when mothers lack support. If a person cannot safely raise a child, then how can one argue that life matters, whether before or after birth? Pro-life and pro-choice arguments are removed from the practical situations women face.

Further, although abortion is legal in the case of rape in many countries, there can often be religious pressure to refuse abortion. For example, in one small village in Brazil, an 11-year-old girl became pregnant after being raped. Her parents supported her decision to abort. Abortion is legal in Brazil in cases of rape. However, the local priest and others strongly opposed the decision. In the end, the family decided not to abort, due to this pressure (Rosado-Nunes, 249).

While this may seem an extreme example, it does not sit alone. For example, Pope John Paul II wrote to an archbishop in Sarajevo suggesting the Croatian women raped during the war by non-Christians should "'accept the enemy' into them" and to make him "the flesh of their own flesh" (Stein, 39–40). War, family, religion, and other structures constrain a woman's choices, even when raped.

In terms of contraception, women can lack choice. Access to contraception is positive; forced contraception is not. New methods of contraception tend to be tested out on poor women, particularly poor women of color. Poor women and women of color are also marginalized around the globe through an attempt to control the population growth of particular races and nationalities.[12] In the USA, Planned Parenthood began its work, closely aligned with eugenics. This raises the question of who should have the right to determine when and if a woman can have a child?

Forced sterilization also occurred among women of color. Rather than being able to make a choice about an individual pregnancy, some women were sterilized, sometimes without their knowledge. This permanent decision was considered a better moral choice than abortion, which is a choice not to have a child but leaves the door open for a later pregnancy.

While women may have a difficult time ending a pregnancy, at the other end of the spectrum is the ability to end a pregnancy if the child is unwanted genetically and if the pregnant woman is wealthy enough. If one can selectively abort a fetus due to disability or gender, it perpetuates the injustice in our society. Access to abortion does not address the underlying structures of inequality and unequal valuing of human life. Could we rethink the way society privileges some over others?

Economic factors constrain which women can have children just as they constrain when women can choose not to have children. For example, wealthy working women can pay for a surrogate to bear their child. This may enable them to continue a career without interruption, avoid bodily changes, avoid pregnancy risk, and so forth. Poor women often do not have this option.

Further, the inequalities persist after a child is born. This fact influences whether a woman can choose to have a child. In the USA, poor women, often migrants, take care of wealthier US women's children. Here, for a minimal wage, the worker cares for the child and usually cooks and cleans. While the US woman is freed from these domestic duties, global inequalities between women increase. Many women from the global South serving as domestic workers must leave their own children, often sending money back to the people caring for the child in the home country, usually extended family.[13] This mimics our US history of using black women as "wet nurses." Black women, slaves or maids, had to set their own children to one side and nurse white women's babies. Black women could not tend to their own children. Further, domestic work is poorly remunerated, remaining undervalued as we analyzed in previous chapters.

Bible

Let's examine what the biblical text and tradition tell us about reproduction. Given there is nothing specific about many reproductive issues in the biblical text, how can the text help us? The Hebrew text focused on procreation. The New Testament highlights celibacy.

The argument for procreation often rests on Genesis 1:28: "God blessed them, and God said to them, 'Be fruitful and multiply, and fill the earth and subdue it.'" David Daube[14] noted that this is a blessing rather than a commandment. When we tell someone to "have a good day," this is not a command but a wish for them. He argues the same is true for the Genesis statement: God gave a blessing, not a command (Carmichael, 2). So if we are not under an order to procreate, what then can we say about reproduction? It was important for the Jewish context of the Hebrew Bible but not for the early Christians, who expected Jesus to return imminently.

Further, there is nothing specific in the biblical text about abortion, contraception, and other technological advances. For example, while Christians may cite Psalm 139:13–16 or Isaiah 44:2, 24 as evidence that life begins before birth, none of these verses state that a fetus is a full person at the moment of conception or why this life should be prioritized over any other. George O'Brien, Catholic philosopher, argues that a baby and a fetus are treated differently within the biblical text, citing Exodus 21:22–25. If a woman was killed, the person who killed her was put to death. If the woman lived but suffered a miscarriage, the attacker was fined (71–72). Even if we grant a literal reading, which many scholars and theologians would counter, there is ambiguity when looking to scripture to determine when the fetus becomes a full person.

One scripture also used in terms of reproduction is Deuteronomy 30:19: "I have set before you life and death, blessing and curse; therefore choose life so that you and your descendants may live." Again, while the choice for life is clear, whose life should be prioritized and when is less clear. I return to this question of life in the theological section.

Christian Tradition

For the early church fathers, including Augustine, sex was for procreation, and should occur within marriage, though celibacy was preferred. One did not have to procreate but it was the only reason to have sex. If a person did not want a child, then that person did not have sex. Catholic Church doctrine on sex stated it had to be open to procreation. In contrast, Protestants have been less dogmatic, particularly as birth control has become an option. Protestant traditions also see marriage as a covenant with God or with God and with the community, to build relations. While Protestantism supports procreation within marriage, it does not require procreation.

Prior to the seventeenth century, abortion was only considered wrong after the fourth month (quickening). This thinking shifted in the seventeenth century, when scientists assumed the sperm from the male was a complete being in and of itself. If the sperm was already a life, it should not be prevented from developing. The female provided the food the sperm needed to grow. Hence, the assumption became that life begins at conception, once the sperm implanted itself into the womb. The woman was not to prevent this implantation. While scientists have moved beyond this notion, many people still assume human life begins at conception. From this perspective, then, ending this life would be sinful.

The Catholic Church, at least lower in the hierarchy, has partially shifted its view on contraception. During Vatican II, a Vatican commission recommended contraception be allowed for couples to enable them to be responsible parents. However, the Pope rejected this recommendation, restating that every act of sex within marriage must be open to procreation. Most Catholic theologians, priests, and laity disagree. Rosemary Ruether, feminist theologian, notes 98% of US Catholic women use contraceptives, with 72% believing this use is acceptable within Catholicism (187). While the Vatican may retain one view, many in the church itself choose another.

The Vatican continues to condemn abortion and sterilization. Even Vatican II, considered a liberalizing force, stated in its summary document: "Life must be protected with the utmost care from the moment of conception: abortion and infanticide are abominable crimes" (Paul IV, 51). The Pope asserted in *Humane Vitae*: "[D]irectly willed and procured abortion, even if for therapeutic reasons, is to be absolutely excluded as licit means of regulating birth. Equally to be excluded … is direct sterilization … similarly excluded is every action which … proposes … to render procreation impossible (14)" (Sjørup, 84). No abortion is permissible; no sterilization; no contraception; and so forth.

The church tended to ignore the advice regarding contraception and sterilization and instead focused on abortion. According to the church, the woman's responsibility is to nurture the fetus, regardless of her situation. The Catholic Church is not, however, as attentive to the humanity of the miscarried fetus, which is a contradiction. If the fetus is a human being, why is there no required baptism, blessing, or burial for either a fertilized embryo or a miscarriage?

Theology

Generally speaking, the Christian tradition focused on rejecting abortion and often critiqued contraception. However, IVF and surrogacy were not addressed. We need a holistic approach to a theology of reproduction.

Our theology needs to begin with the reality of marginalized women. As Ivone Gebara[15] states, "[m]oral principles are important, but what does any principle mean when today, at this moment, you are pregnant and you have nothing to nourish your three or four children already birthed?" (Gebara 1995, 132). What theology would emerge from this reality? What decisions would be made?

Thinking theologically, there is no need to reproduce or attach reproduction to marriage. Instead, reproductive justice is a communal issue, a structural issue. For ecofeminists the key is not an individual but persons and their relations with each other. We are connected with the earth and all humans in it. Human beings and nature are to be respected because all life is sacred. We need to take into account the variety of lives at stake and how best to support life in general in all our decisions. These decisions involve each person: male, female, intersex, adult and child, the wider family, the wider community. A woman does not get pregnant alone and does not raise a child alone. Thinking about reproduction as a community decision may lead to different action.

A new reproductive ethic could be formed. This ethic could consider reproduction in terms of community. Our current priorities are unethical. We are racist, sexist, classist, and so forth. Unethical means we fail to remember we are in relation with other creatures on the planet. We need to respect all creatures, human and otherwise. Many women have to choose between lives. Bringing a child into the world is not inherently positive. Sometimes protecting life means protecting the lives of those already born. Thus, not having a child can be a good decision.

We need to shift our structures so people can actually choose to bring a child into the world. In our current global society, often a woman cannot choose whether or not to get pregnant, to give birth, or to raise a child. We need first to alter our structures to choose life, to support the lives of those already with us. To prioritize life, people must first be able to raise any children they do have. The woman breastfeeding while drinking alcohol is set within a wider web of relations that led to her situation. The wealthy woman choosing surrogacy is set within the wider spectrum of inequality around the globe. A theology focused on relatedness recognizes that white wealthy women have been prioritized over others and works to undo this privilege.

Part of this more global understanding of a network of relations is rethinking parental "ownership" of children. When we speak about the children we've had, we usually talk about them as "mine," as if children are possessions. Now while most of us would deny a literal sense of ownership, we do tend to want to mold them in some way. The extreme version of this molding is fetal selection. However, children are gifts to us from God, shared. Only God can claim ownership over anything.

Our sense of owning our children is dangerous. We tend to treat children as an investment or an experiment. I've had several students state that they had to choose a particular major, or even attend college, because their parents had invested so much in them. I've had students say their parents always planned for them to be a doctor. Where is the perspective of the child in this? Further, do we want the best for all children or just our own child(ren)?

In fact, children are strangers to us. We agree to raise them, whether biological or adopted. According to Christian Scripture, the relationship of God with the wider human community is adoptive. God made a covenant with the Jewish people. Then, through Jesus, Christianity states that God extended this covenant to all. As Christians, we have been adopted into God's family, even if many of us were "born" into Christian families. We are each adopted. What could this understanding mean for reproduction in general? The new child who enters the world is either adopted or abandoned by that world. Each of us is responsible for the children who enter the world.

How could we shift our understanding to take communal responsibility for reproduction and the raising of children? More work needs to be done in this area.

Act

Lest we downplay the necessary structural change, Andrea Smith suggests, "a reproductive justice agenda must make the dismantling of capitalism, white supremacy, and colonialism central to its agenda" (Smith 2005, 135). Each of these changes is needed for women to be able to choose to bear children and choose to raise their children safely.

In terms of possible actions, I draw on the work of Gebara, SisterSong, Smith, and Janet Jakobsen[16] for the following suggestions:

1. Recognize society is abortive. Gebara argued that daily life in Brazil, her context, is continuously abortive.[17] People are constantly harmed and killed, not just in Brazil but across the globe. Societal abortion should be overcome before any discussion of abortion itself. Hence, abortion should be legal at least until societal abortion ends.
2. Recognize that raising children is a communal responsibility.
3. Globally, work to ensure women have and can use their human rights (SisterSong in Sidun 110).
4. Work to ensure women can decide how many children to have and when to have them (SisterSong in Sidun 110). This work would include safe and affordable health care and child care for all, among other things. Within the USA, this work would include a shift in welfare policies.
5. Ensure parents can safely and healthily raise their children (SisterSong in Sidun 110). The previous concept detailed how.

6. Ensure everyone can live healthily and safely (SisterSong in Sidun, 110). This shift would include the freedom for each person to choose whom to have sex with and when, as well as an end to all oppression.
7. Within the USA and outside, dangerous contraceptives should not be promoted.
8. Further, pregnant women with problems such as addiction should be supported, not criminalized.

Each person should have reproductive rights and responsibilities, as individuals and communities. The focus should be on creating a safe and healthy environment for all people.

Moving Forward

From a liberationist perspective, God is on the side of women of color, poor women, and their fetuses. When any person cannot choose to have and raise a child in a safe environment, that is a sin committed by us all. We are all responsible for creating a safe world where each person can live freely and fully.

From birth until at least into the teenage years, children are dependent on us for many if not all their needs. Children must be supported within the community. Giving birth to a child is not creating ownership of a child but bringing another human being into the world, belonging to God. We all share in the responsibility of raising children. Having children is not about continuing a family line or ensuring our genes remain on the earth. It is about building community.

Thus, any decision about reproduction rests in the larger decisions we make about our society, how we treat each person in our society, in our global community. It is about creating the world we want children to have. To move toward reproductive justice, we need to reflect and act on all aspects of reproduction.

Questions for Reflection

1. How would you define reproductive justice? To what extent do you think it exists now?
2. What, for you, would be the most important shift we could make in society toward reproductive justice?

3. I have argued that reproductive issues should be considered separately from sexual relationships. To what extent do you agree or disagree?

Further Suggested Reading

Gebara, Ivone. 1995 'The Abortion Debate in Brazil: A Report from an Ecofeminist Philosopher Under Siege,' *Journal of Feminist Studies in Religion*, 11, no 2, 129–35.

Gebara's article presented the revolutionary view that daily life in Brazil was itself abortive and thus the conversation around abortion needed to be reframed to take into account that poor women in Brazil (and elsewhere) could not protect the lives of their already-born children, rendering the abortion debate moot. Silenced by the Vatican for her writing, her ecofeminist stance remains an important perspective on the issue of reproductive justice.

Norsworthy, K., M. McLaren, and L. Waterfield. 2012 'Women's Power in Relationships: A Matter of Social Justice.' In *Reproductive Justice: A Global Concern.* ed, J. Chrisler. Denver: Praeger: 57–75.

This excellent chapter details varied understandings of power and how power affects women's choice in terms of what relationships they have and what decisions they can make within those relationships and within society at large. It articulates the constraints that either empower or disempower women in their ability to make reproductive choices.

Smith, Andrea. 2005 'Beyond Pro-Choice Versus Pro-Life: Women of Color and Reproductive Justice,' *NWSA Journal*, Vol. 17, No. 1 (Spring).

Smith's article argues that situating the abortion debate in terms of life or choice marginalizes many women. Instead, she argues for a structural approach to reproductive justice that prioritizes those often left out: the poor, women of color, people with disabilities, and so forth.

NOTES

1. This is an understatement according to data from the Centers for Disease Control and Prevention (CDC). In the statistics from 2010, they estimate the abortion rate to be 8.6 for white women, 31.8 for black women, 18.6 for Hispanic, and 16 for others, with an overall abortion rate of 14.4. The abortion rate is "number of abortions obtained by women in a given race/ethnicity group per 1000 women in that same group" (Pazol et al., 31).

2. Andrea Smith is a feminist scholar focused on Native American women.
3. See Stormer.
4. See Roberts.
5. California, Connecticut, Delaware, Georgia, Illinois, Iowa, Louisiana, Maryland, Mississippi, Ohio, South Carolina, Tennessee, and Virginia.
6. "Sterilization rates went as high as 80 percent in some tribes" (Smith 1995, 42).
7. "In 2009, 29 percent of countries permitted abortion on request ...; 97 percent of countries permitted abortion to save a woman's life, 67 percent to preserve physical health, and 63 percent to preserve mental health. Rape or incest and fetal impairment were slightly less common at 49 percent and 47 percent, respectively. Thirty-four percent permitted abortion for economic or social reasons (UN 2011b). The majority of countries with highly restrictive laws were in the developing world, particularly in Africa and Latin America where 92–97 percent of women live under restrictive abortion laws (Singh et al. 2009)" (Russo and Steinberg, 161).
8. "The responsibilities of mothers having abortions were substantial: 61% of such Black mothers had more than one child; 53% of such White mothers had more than one child" (Russo and Dabul, 25).
9. "Of the 194 Black women who had had at least one abortion, 86% were mothers; for the 398 Black women with no history of abortion, the figure was 65%" (Russo and Dabul, 25). In contrast, "of the 527 White women who had had at least one abortion, 302 (57%) were mothers; for the 1402 White women with no history of abortion, 53% were mothers" (Russo and Dabul, 25).
10. See http://www.bbc.com/news/uk-23721893
11. See http://online.wsj.com/news/articles/SB122230566090673837 for details of cases upheld and overturned. See also http://www.abajournal.com/mobile/article/appeals_court_overturns_judge_who_ordered_sterilization_for_schizophrenic_p/ for details of a sterilization order overturned by an appeals court. Finally, see also http://news.yahoo.com/mans-plea-deal-includes-vasectomy-requirement-191927115.html for details of a plea agreement that involved a vasectomy for a reduced prison sentence.
12. See Hartmann.
13. See Ehrenreich and Hochschild (2002).
14. Daube was a German scholar of biblical and Roman law who lived from 1909 to 1999.
15. Ivone Gebara is a Brazilian nun and feminist liberation theologian.
16. Jakobsen is a professor of Women, Gender, and Sexuality Studies at Barnard College.

17. "I live in a poor neighborhood-Camaragibe, in the state of Pernambuco, in the northeast of Brazil. I have learned how hard it is to speak about 'choices,' much less to assume that women have or can have 'free choice.' Most often poor women have *no* choice, and they certainly are not ... They are forced to live in poverty, to eat whatever they can obtain, to work at whatever they can find. Most of them never use the word *freedom.* They speak readily of slavery" (Gebara 1995, 130). "Legalization of abortion is, then, merely one goal within a broader struggle to overcome an already deeply abortive society. Poor conditions in housing, diet, employment, and health care, as well as the absence of conditions of sustainable life, are the signs of continuous social abortion in daily life" (Gebara 1995, 131).

References

Carmichael, C. 2010. *Sex & Religion in the Bible.* New Haven: Yale University Press.

Ehrenreich, Barbara, and Arlie Hochschild. 2002. *Global Woman: Nannies, Maids, and Sex Workers in the New Economy.* New York: Holt Paperbacks.

Gebara, Ivone. 1995. The Abortion Debate in Brazil: A Report from an Ecofeminist Philosopher Under Siege. *Journal of Feminist Studies in Religion* 11 (2): 129–135.

Goldkamp, R. 2011. Bumping Heads over Race and Abortion. *Human Life Review* 2011: 81–85.

Hartman, Betsy. 1995. *Reproductive Rights and Wrongs: The Global Politics of Population Control.* Boston: South End Press.

Jones, R., and K. Kooistra. 2011. Abortion Incidence and Access to Services in the United States, 2008. *Perspectives on Sexual and Reproductive Health* 43 (1): 41–50. https://www.guttmacher.org/pubs/journals/4304111.pdf. Accessed 1 Sept 2014.

Nelson, J. 2003. *Women of color and the reproductive rights movement.* New York: New York University Press.

Norsworthy, K., M. McLaren, and L. Waterfield. 2012. Women's Power in Relationships: A Matter of Social Justice. In *Reproductive Justice: A Global Concern*, ed. J. Chrisler, 57–75. Denver: Praeger.

O'Brien, G. 2010. *The Church and Abortion: A Catholic Dissent.* New York: Rowman & Littlefield.

Pazol, K. et al. 2010. Abortion Surveillance – United States, 2010. In *Surveillance Summaries.* https://www.cdc.gov/mmwr/preview/mmwrhtml/ss6208a1.htm. Accessed 31 Oct 2017.

Pope Paul VI. 1965. *Gaudium et Spes.* http://www.vatican.va/archive/hist_councils/ii_vatican_council/documents/vat-ii_cons_19651207_gaudium-et-spes_en.html. Accessed 3 Sept 2014.

Roberts, Dorothy. 1997. *Killing the Black Body: Race, Reproduction, and the Meaning of Liberty*. New York: Pantheon.

Rosado-Nunes, M. 2010. Catholicism and Women's Rights as Human Rights In *Hope Abundant: Third World and Indigenous Women's Theology*, ed. Kwok Pui-lan, 241–254. Maryknoll: Orbis Books.

Rubin, L., and A. Phillips. 2012. Infertility and Assisted Reproductive Technologies: Matters of Reproductive Justice. In *Reproductive Justice: A Global Concern*, ed. J. Chrisler, 173–199. Denver: Praeger.

Ruether, Rosemary. 2008. Women, Reproductive Rights and the Catholic Church. *Feminist Theology* 16 (2): 184–193.

Russo, N., and A. Dabul. 1997. The Relationship of Abortion to Well-Being: Do Race and Religion Make a Difference? *Professional Psychology: Research and Practice* 28 (1): 23–31.

Russo, N., and J. Steinberg. 2012. Contraception and Abortion: Critical Tools for Achieving Reproductive Justice. In *Reproductive Justice: A Global Concern*, ed. J. Chrisler, 145–172. Denver: Praeger.

Sidun, N. 2012. Reproductive Injustice: The Trafficking and Sexual Exploitation of Women and Girls. In *Reproductive Justice: A Global Concern*, ed. J. Chrisler, 93–115. Denver: Praeger.

Sjørup, L. 1999. The Vatican and Women's Reproductive Health and Rights: A Clash of Civilizations? *Feminist Theology* 21: 79–97.

Smith, Andrea. 1995. Women of Color and Reproductive Choice: Combating the Population Paradigm. *Journal of Feminist Studies in Religion* 11 (2): 39–66.

———. 2005. Beyond Pro-Choice Versus Pro-Life: Women of Color and Reproductive Justice. *NWSA Journal* 17 (1): 119–140 (Spring).

Stein, D. 1995. *People Who Count: Population and Politics, Women and Children*. London: Earthscan.

Stormer, N. 2002. *Articulating Life's Memory: U.S. Medical Rhetoric About Abortion in the Nineteenth Century*. Lanham: Lexington Books.

CHAPTER 7

Conclusion

Abstract The conclusion draws together the main threads of the book, arguing that good sex takes effort, action, and reflection but in this work humans come to know God. To have good sex, one needs to redefine desire and sex as positive aspects of human creation. Understanding sex as a way to know God upends our perspective on marriage, sex work, and reproduction, challenging us to work toward a more just world.

Keywords Desire • Sex • Partnership • Sex work • Reproduction

This book approached sexual theology from the perspective of those most marginalized to articulate how to have good sex. Our first step to creating a healthy sexual ethic is to recognize that sex is not inherently sinful. Desire is not inherently sinful. The negative aspect of desire is assuming possession is the goal. The negative aspect of sex is holding power over another. Sin lies in the structures of racism, sexism, heterosexism, and so forth that privilege some over others, creating unjust relations. Addressing desire and sex requires attention to the body, power, and violence. It requires thinking about such varied contexts as partnership, sex work, and reproduction.

T. Cooper, *A Christian Guide to Liberating Desire, Sex, Partnership, Work, and Reproduction*,
https://doi.org/10.1007/978-3-319-70896-6_7

To achieve reproductive justice, we need to acknowledge that in our society sex and reproduction need not be connected. Instead, we can consider reproduction in a community context, where we all share responsibility for children. We need to create structures enabling people to have and raise children if and when they choose. We can no longer prioritize white wealthy people over others. We can assess sex separately.

To have just sex work, we need to stop condemning people who buy, sell, and manage in the trade. Instead, we can work from the perspective of people in the trade to make it just. Our structures should change so no one need work in the trade but people who choose to can be safe and have good sex. At least in the current sex trade, money is exchanged, and in our unjust society, there is a small measure of power. Marriage, considering wives as property, has been worse and not condemned.

In terms of partnership, we need to stop prioritizing marriage, an exclusive institution dividing more than it unites, privileging white wealthy people. Instead, we should focus on healthy relationships and craft societal structures to support those relationships, whatever they may look like. We also need to develop a theology of friendship.

We can have good sex. Good sex is consensual, mutual, and pleasurable. Our unjust society makes it difficult to create contexts for good sex. Hence, we need to change the structures to support healthy sexual relationships.

In terms of desire, we need to acknowledge that desire is God-given. Our desire stems from wanting to know God. Such desire, sexual or otherwise, will encourage us to know others, to empower others. We need to change our structures to support this notion.

In summary, good sex takes effort, action, and reflection but in this work and play we come to know God.

Three Last Questions for Reflection

The theological framework for the issues considered in this book may have been new to you.

1. What two to three concepts have resonated with you that you could integrate into your daily life?
2. What two to three concepts are you wrestling with that you want to dig into further? (You could start with the further suggested reading at the end of the relevant chapters. You can also be in touch with me for further readings.)
3. Can sex be a way to know God? Why or why not?

Definitions

Gender	Gender refers to the cultural characteristics that we often assign to particular biological sex. Thus, men are "masculine" and women are "feminine." Gender and sex are assumed to go together. However, gender is also a spectrum. People who are born male and take on a male identity and people who are born female and assume a female identity are known as **cisgender**. People whose sex and gender do not coincide are known as **transgender**. There are also many people who do not adhere to all the gender traits assigned to their biological sex. Our difficulty in dealing with this complexity is shown even with children at a young age, for example, if a boy wants to wear a dress and/or nail polish or if a girl plays with trucks and cars.
Sex	One's "sex" refers to the biology of a human with regard to reproductive organs and hormones. Sex is usually assigned at birth based on the dominant organs. Although we tend to separate the sexes into male and female, people can be born with both male and female reproductive organs. People can also be born with the genitalia of one sex and the dominant hormones of the

T. Cooper, *A Christian Guide to Liberating Desire, Sex, Partnership, Work, and Reproduction*,
https://doi.org/10.1007/978-3-319-70896-6

	other. So while dominant culture separates us into males and females, there is actually a spectrum. Neither sex nor gender can be assumed from one's appearance. Further, there is a movement to end assigning sex at birth, since some of the biological characteristics are not clear until later in childhood.
Sexual Health	"A state of physical, emotional, mental and social well-being in relation to sexuality, and not merely the absence of disease, dysfunction or infirmity. Sexual health requires a positive and respectful approach to sexuality and sexual relationships, as well as the possibility of having pleasurable and safe sexual experiences, free of coercion, discrimination, and violence" (WHO, 5).
Sexual Identity	Sexual identity is a combination of our biological sex, our gender, and our orientation.
Sexual Orientation	Sexual orientation denotes who an individual is attracted to. We may be heterosexual: attracted to the opposite sex and gender. We may be homosexual: attracted to the same sex and gender. We may be bisexual: attracted to varying sexes and genders. And since sex and gender are also spectrums: we may not fit into a particular label in our attractions.
Sexuality	Sexuality is the process of coming to know and sharing your sex, gender, and orientation. Dynamic rather than static, it is a component in all relationships. We are sexual beings whether or not we choose to act on our sexuality. Sexuality is negotiated within each relationship and in the society at large.
Sexual Poverty	Sexual poverty is the inability, due to societal constructs, of being our true sexual selves. It is caused by injustice, and the imbalance of sexual power between individuals and within structures. A clear example of sexual poverty would be a rape victim. So too would be the partner in a relationship who feels pressured to engage in sexually with the other. In our unjust society, there are aspects of dominance and submission in all relationships but the crucial element is power or lack thereof. Sexual poverty often intersects with other forms of poverty.

Further References

Althaus-Reid, Marcella, ed. 2006. *Liberation Theology and Sexuality*. Aldershot: Ashgate.

Bartkowski, J., A. Ramos-Wada, C. Ellison, and G. Acevedo. 2012. Faith, Race-Ethnicity, and Public Policy Preferences: Religious Schemas and Abortion Attitudes Among U.S. Latinos. *Journal for the Scientific Study of Religion* 51 (2): 343–358.

Boer, Roland. 2012. *The Earthy Nature of the Bible: Fleshly Readings of Sex, Masculinity, and Carnality*. New York: Palgrave.

Cannon, Katie Geneva. 2010. Sexing Black Women: Liberation from the Prisonhouse of Anatomical Authority. In *Sexuality and the Sacred*, ed. Marvin M. Ellison and Kelly Brown Douglas, 2nd ed., 78–94. Louisville: Westminster John Knox Press.

Cattoi, Thomas, and June McDaniel, eds. 2011. *Perceiving the Divine Through the Human Body: Mystical Sensuality*. New York: Palgrave Macmillan.

Cheng, Patrick. 2010. Rethinking Sin and Grace for LGBT People Today. In *Sexuality and the Sacred*, ed. Marvin M. Ellison and Kelly Brown Douglas, 2nd ed., 105–118. Louisville: Westminster John Knox Press.

Chrisler, J., ed. 2012. *Reproductive Justice: A Global Concern*. Denver: Praeger.

DeConick, April. 2011. *Holy Misogyny: Why the Sex and Gender Conflicts in the Early Church Still Matter*. New York: Continuum.

Douglas, Kelly Brown. 2010. Black and Blues: God-Talk/Body-Talk for the Black Church. In *Sexuality and the Sacred*, ed. Marvin M. Ellison and Kelly Brown Douglas, 2nd ed., 48–68. Louisville: Westminster John Knox Press.

T. Cooper, *A Christian Guide to Liberating Desire, Sex, Partnership, Work, and Reproduction*,
https://doi.org/10.1007/978-3-319-70896-6

Ellison, M.M. 2010. Reimagining Good Sex: The Eroticizing of Mutual Respect and Pleasure. In *Sexuality and the Sacred*, ed. Marvin M. Ellison and Kelly Brown Douglas, 2nd ed., 245–261. Louisville: Westminster John Knox Press.

Farley, Margaret. 2006. *Just Love: A Framework for Christian Sexual Ethics*. New York: Continuum.

Foucault, Michel. 1990. *The Use of Pleasure: Volume 2 of the History of Sexuality*. New York: Vintage Books.

Gardner, Christine. 2011. *Making Chastity Sexy: The Rhetoric of Evangelical Abstinence Campaigns*. Berkeley: University of California Press.

Hunt, S.J., and A.K.T. Yip, eds. 2012. *The Ashgate Research Companion to Contemporary Religion and Sexuality*. Burlington: Ashgate.

Isherwood, Lisa, and Mark D. Jordan, eds. 2010. *Dancing Theology in Fetish Boots: Essays in Honour of Marcella Althaus-Reid*. London: SCM Press.

Jarman, Michelle. 2012. Dismembering the Lynch Mob: Intersecting Narratives of Disability, Race, and Sexual Menace. In *Sex and Disability*, ed. Robert McRuer and Anna Mollow, 89–107. Durham: Duke University Press.

Jung, Patricia Beattie, and Aana Marie Vigen, eds. 2010. *God, Science, Sex, Gender: An Interdisciplinary Approach to Christian Ethics*. Chicago: University of Illinois Press.

Kline, W. 2010. *Bodies of Knowledge: Sexuality, Reproduction, and Women's Health in the Second Wave*. Chicago: University of Chicago Press.

McCarthy, David Matzko. 2001. *Sex & Love in the Home*. London: SCM Press.

McCleneghan, Bromleigh. 2016. *Good Christian Sex: Why Chastity Isn't the Only Option – And Other Things the Bible Says About Sex*. San Francisco: HarperOne.

Mohanty, C. 2003. *Feminism Without Borders: Decolonizing Theory, Practicing Solidarity*. Durham: Duke University Press.

Moulaison, Jane Barter. 2010. Bodies Without Borders: Desire, Abjection, and Human Sexuality in Recent Theology. In *Human Sexuality and the Nuptial Mystery*, ed. Roy Jeal, 65–82. Eugene: Cascade Books.

Nancy, Jean Luc. 2013. *Corpus II. Writings on Sexuality*. Trans. Anne O'Byrne. New York: Fordham University Press.

Nelson, J. 2003. *Women of Color and the Reproductive Rights Movement*. New York: New York University Press.

Nynäs, Peter, and Andrew Kam-Tuck Yip, eds. 2012. *Religion, Gender and Sexuality in Everyday Life*. Burlington: Ashgate.

Ott, Kate. 2013. *Sex + Faith: Talking with Your Child from Birth to Adolescence*. Louisville: Westminster John Knox.

Price, K. 2010. What is Reproductive Justice? How Women of Color Activists are Redefining the Pro-choice Paradigm. *Meridians: Feminism, Race, Transnationalism* 10 (2): 42–65.

Sahni, Rohini, V. Kalyan Shankar, and Hemant Apte, eds. 2008. *Prostitution and Beyond: An Analysis of Sex Work in India*. Thousand Oaks: Sage.

Simien, E., and R. Clawson. 2004. The Intersection of Race and Gender: An Examination of Black Feminist Consciousness, Race Consciousness, and Policy Attitudes. *Social Science Quarterly* 85 (3): 793–810.

Sung, J.M. 2007. *Desire, Market and Religion*. London: SCM Press.

Index[1]

A

Abortion, 94, 95, 97–103, 105, 107n1, 108n6, 108n7, 108n8, 108n9, 109n17
Abstinence, 48
Abuse, 9, 17, 65, 66, 75n4, 86, 90, 94
Adultery, 59, 63, 66, 75n2, 81
Agape, 24, 71, 72
Augustine, St., 14, 15, 20n12, 30, 47, 69, 71, 72, 102

B

Bible, 10–14, 19, 25, 29–31, 46, 49, 67–69, 71, 74, 75n2, 80, 86, 92n4, 101, 102, 108n14
  See also New Testament
Bodies, 5–10, 12, 14, 16, 18, 23, 25, 26, 28, 30, 33, 36–38, 41, 45, 48–50, 52, 55n8, 69, 80, 86, 88, 94, 95, 111

C

Capitalism, 26, 43, 83, 86, 90, 105
Catholic Church, 15, 70, 76n7, 93, 102, 103
Celibacy, 12, 14, 46, 47, 68–70, 87, 101, 102
Children, 3, 11–14, 17, 19n2, 20n9, 30, 38, 39, 43, 47, 49, 59, 61, 62, 65, 69, 70, 74, 81, 86, 87, 89, 93–96, 98–106, 108n8, 112
Classism, 29, 32, 36, 52, 74, 87, 90, 99
Communion, 13, 16–18, 29, 30, 32, 45, 49–51, 53, 54, 72
Consent, 8, 45, 47, 50, 52, 53, 58, 66, 68, 69, 73, 82, 89, 96
Contraception, 13, 94–97, 100–103
Covenant, 29, 31, 53, 71, 73, 102, 105

[1] Note: Page number followed by 'n' refers to notes.

T. Cooper, *A Christian Guide to Liberating Desire, Sex, Partnership, Work, and Reproduction*,
https://doi.org/10.1007/978-3-319-70896-6

D
David, 12
Desire, 7, 8, 11–18, 20n6, 23–33, 35–40, 42–49, 51, 53, 54, 55n8, 57–59, 62–65, 68–70, 72, 74, 79, 80, 82–84, 87, 89, 99, 111, 112
Disability, 44, 94, 96, 98–100
Divorce, 12, 59
Dominance, 8–10, 25, 44, 45

E
Empowerment, 8, 17, 18, 20n8, 27
Eros, 28, 29, 31, 32, 40, 71, 72
Eucharist, 49, 50, 55n8
Eve, 14, 29, 30, 68, 87
Exploitation, 17, 81, 83, 85, 88, 90

F
Friendship, 27, 41, 57, 58, 62, 65–69, 71–74, 112

G
Gender, 3–7, 9, 17, 63–66, 80, 82, 84, 85, 100, 108n16

H
Hebrew Bible, 25, 29, 46, 49, 68, 69, 101
Heterosexism, 36, 52, 86, 87, 90, 111
Homosexuality, 6, 25, 37, 39, 57, 84
Honesty, 66–68, 73, 74, 83

I
Injustice, 5, 17, 29, 40, 88, 96, 100
Intercourse, 15, 36, 37, 46–48, 50, 63, 69, 70, 74, 80, 86
Intimacy, 7, 40, 51, 53, 64, 66, 75n5, 80

J
Jesus, 7, 11, 12, 14, 16, 18, 29–31, 49, 50, 55n8, 55n9, 68, 72, 79, 80, 86, 88, 101, 105
Judaism, 58, 71, 86
Justice, 1, 3, 10, 11, 14, 16, 28, 32, 36, 46, 51, 52, 54, 72, 74, 88, 90, 93, 103, 105, 106

L
Love, 2, 9, 12, 15, 17, 18, 24, 25, 28–30, 32, 36, 42, 44, 45, 51, 52, 54, 60, 63, 66, 68, 71–73

M
Marriage, 1, 2, 5–7, 9, 11–17, 20n5, 25–28, 30, 35–40, 43, 47, 48, 50, 51, 57–74, 75n3, 75n5, 76n6, 79, 87, 91, 93, 102, 103, 112
Mary, 11, 12, 46, 47
Masculinity, 8, 9, 17
Masturbation, 38, 40, 70
Mutuality, 9, 10, 45, 50, 52, 53, 58, 67, 68, 73, 74, 86

N
New Testament, 7, 11, 20n10, 25, 29–31, 44, 46, 59, 68, 86, 101
See also Bible

O
Openness, 41, 45, 64
Oppression, 5, 84–86, 93, 106
Orgasm, 37–42, 45, 46, 49

P
Partnership, 11, 12, 18, 26, 27, 32, 34n4, 51, 54, 111, 112
Patriarchy, 3, 42, 44, 45, 64, 84

Paul, 12, 30, 34n5, 46, 68
Possession, 23, 26–29, 31, 32, 35, 104, 111
Power, 2, 3, 6, 7, 17, 18, 20n7, 20n8, 26–29, 31, 36, 42–45, 50, 52–54, 64, 73, 81, 82, 85, 86, 89, 98, 111, 112
Pregnancy, 60, 74, 95, 97, 98, 100, 101
Privilege, 5, 53, 58, 60, 64, 73, 100, 104, 111
Procreation, 7, 11, 12, 14–17, 30, 35–40, 42, 44, 46–48, 59–62, 68–71, 81, 93–95, 101–103
Prostitution, 43, 80, 81, 83, 86–88
Protestantism, 15, 70, 102

R

Racism, 5, 26, 29, 32, 36, 39, 40, 52, 61, 64, 74, 86, 87, 90, 95, 97, 99, 111
Rahab, 12, 86, 92n5
Rape, 5, 9, 10, 17, 39, 65, 66, 75n4, 75n5, 82, 89, 98, 100, 108n7
Reproduction, 5, 12, 18, 27, 43, 74, 93–107
Ruth, 12, 46, 86, 92n6

S

Sex, 1–19, 26–28, 30, 32, 33, 35–55, 57–70, 72–74, 75n2, 75n4, 79, 93–98, 102, 103, 106, 111, 112
Sexism, 29, 32, 52, 74, 86, 87, 90, 99, 111
Sex work, 18, 27, 79–91, 111, 112
Sin, 14, 15, 17, 30, 31, 47, 48, 60, 73, 87, 88, 90, 106, 111
Slavery, 5, 16, 25, 28, 39, 57, 80, 82, 83, 96, 109n17
Song of Songs, 12, 29, 46, 50
Sterilization, 94–97, 100, 103, 108n6, 108n11
Surrogacy, 94, 99, 103, 104

T

Trinity, 30, 31, 72
Trust, 32, 41, 53

V

Violence, 6, 7, 17, 36, 38, 40, 44, 60, 64, 66, 75n4, 82, 90, 111
Vulnerability, 7, 45, 64

CPSIA information can be obtained
at www.ICGtesting.com
Printed in the USA
LVHW080432040123
736325LV00007B/467

9 783319 708959